Love to you at Christmas. Graham.
Barbie 1991. X.

Love to you at Christmas. Graham.
Barbie 1991. X.

Images
of
WIRRAL

Images
of
WIRRAL

A celebration in words and photographs
of a unique peninsula

KENNETH BURNLEY
&
GUY HUNTINGTON

THE SILVER BIRCH PRESS
WIRRAL · CHESHIRE

First published in Great Britain 1991
by the Silver Birch Press, 248 Telegraph Road, Heswall, Wirral, L61 7SG

ISBN 0 9517961 0 0

Printed by Printfine Ltd,
Gibraltar Row,
King Edward Industrial Estate,
Liverpool L3 7HJ

This book is dedicated to the countless folk who, down the ages,
have helped make Wirral such a beautiful and fascinating place.
We particularly acknowledge the work of
the many voluntary groups who are committed to
protecting and improving our unique heritage of countryside and coast,
town, village and estuary.

On a more personal note, we also acknowledge the patience and
forbearance of our respective families, particularly our wives,
who took our many jaunts into the wilds of Wirral with good heart,
and always had a cup of coffee ready on our return!

KENNETH BURNLEY & GUY HUNTINGTON

Contents

VILLAGE & COUNTRY IMAGES

INTRODUCTION

Wirral is a rather special place. First of all, it's a peninsula, and there aren't too many of those around. Two of Britain's great rivers, the Mersey and the Dee, sweep along its eastern and western edges; and the waters of the Irish Sea lap its northern coast. Then, it adjoins two of Britain's great cities, Chester and Liverpool - so different in character, yet each contributing something to the history and development of Wirral. Lastly, within its small area lies a wealth of beauty and interest - busy towns and quiet villages, wild coasts and wooded countryside; seaside and suburbs, wind-swept heathland and flowery meadows.

Wirral has been my home since childhood: for forty years I have been exploring its lanes and byways, its field-paths and bridle-ways, its countryside and coast, and of course, its fascinating history. I live here because I love the place. I never tire of its scenery, its heritage, and its people - the folk of yesterday and today who have contributed something to its life and colour. That's why I wrote this book: to share some of the magic of Wirral with others, in word-images and picture-images.

Images of Wirral is a distinctly personal view of a small corner of England - small in size but great in interest. You will find here images of the Wirral peninsula in all its endless variety - towns and villages, churches and cottages, marshes and meres, docks and dunes. It is a picture of Wirral today, with just a glimpse into its rich past. If in 50 years' time folk look back at this work and say 'Wasn't Wirral beautiful then' it will be a sad thing; for it is my hope that, through this book, people will realise that we have in Wirral something precious to look after, for future generations to enjoy as much as we enjoy it today. If it helps us to make our peninsula an even better place in which to live, I shall be delighted.

This is no history book - Wirral's history has been well told over the years. There *are* historical references throughout the book, but they form only a small part of the text. Folk wishing to find out more about Wirral's history can consult the many published works listed in the Bibliography.

I have divided *Images of Wirral* into four areas: Sea Images, Dee Images, Mersey Images, Village & Country Images; for that is how I see our peninsula. Most places fall into one or other of these groups, but some places could fit into several groups, and the final choice is based on my own personal perception of a place.

If you are a Wirral resident, I hope you will enjoy reading about and seeing your favourite places in a new light. If you have never been to Wirral, perhaps this book will convey to you some of the richness of this oft-neglected and little-known corner of England. And for Wirral exiles living far away, at home or abroad, these words and photographs will, hopefully, bring back happy memories of your home patch and remind you of the beauty and fascination of this land between the Mersey and the Dee.

A word or two about the photographs: it takes a rare and extremely talented person to really capture the richness, variety and beauty of a place like Wirral in visual form. Guy Huntington, who is also Wirral-born and bred, and shares with me that same love for our peninsula, has produced in this book a collection of photographic images which ideally complement my word-images. His expert eye and camera have recorded images of Wirral in all their variety, richness and colour. Together, we hope that you will enjoy this personal celebration of this unique and fascinating peninsula, as much as we have enjoyed creating it.

Kenneth Burnley, July 1991

SEA IMAGES

---

*The feel of the sea pervades Wirral. Its briny tang is carried across the villages,
fields and hedgerows by the eternal breeze which blows in from these northern
waters. The very shape of Wirral has been determined by these watery forces
which, over the centuries, have at times robbed the peninsula of land and,
at other times, given it back.*

*The sea has, in past times, given Wirral folk both food and work;
it has taken them to far-off lands; and it has brought them home again.
It has also seen loss and tragedy, throwing lives, vessels and cargoes to its
watery depths, or casting them without care upon its sandy shores.
Love it or hate it, you cannot ignore it.
It has always been, and always will be, one of the most powerful
images of Wirral.*

NEW BRIGHTON

The ever-popular resort at the mouth of the Mersey estuary

New Brighton? I love the place. I have defended her, and will always defend her, when people (most of whom, I suspect, have rarely been here) denigrate her. During recent years, when it has been fashionable to knock the resort, I have read about the 'dereliction of New Brighton' with disbelief. For this is the same place where, on fine Sundays, winter and summer, people throng the promenade; cars queue for parking-spaces; and the place sings with life and vitality. Perhaps it's not quite what James Atherton had in mind for New Brighton 150 years ago, but I'm sure he would not have been too displeased by the resort of today.

Atherton, a retired Liverpool merchant, was certainly a man of vision. He had to be. Who else would have considered transforming the sandy waste, which covered this corner of the Wirral peninsula in the 1830s, into a watering-place which would become 'a most agreeable and desirable place of resort to the Nobility and Gentry of all the neighbouring counties.'? It was, of course, becoming fashionable to 'take the waters' around our coasts; and in Wirral, with coasts a-plenty, Parkgate had already seen the potential for this new-fangled leisure activity.

The long and colourful history of the development of New Brighton has been well chronicled; it seems to have been a series of perpetual ups and downs. At the turn of the century a local writer commented 'New Brighton has altered greatly for the worse, and again for the better, during the past century; it became a place of residence and then fell on degenerate days, when a huge and ugly terrace of cheap lodging-houses was erected, and the sands were disfigured with all kinds of cheap shows suitable to the Chowbent cheap-tripper. But in these later days it has again taken its place as a residence by the sea, and its shores are again pleasant to walk on.'

These words may well have been written today, for indeed the shores of New Brighton are again pleasant to walk on. Gone, alas, are the tower (at 562 feet, higher than Blackpool's), fairground and open-air pool. Gone too is the pier, but seaside piers are ugly things anyway, and this was no loss to the resort. But it *does* have a fine lighthouse perched on the old Black Rock; and a real fort which, although never used for military purposes, was built to protect the Mersey from the threat of invasion by Napoleon 150 years ago.

But New Brighton's greatest asset is undoubtedly its fine coastal promenade, giving the visitor an unbroken walk of some three miles from the Mersey estuary, around Rock Point towards Harrison Drive. Gone are the days when this scene was 'enlivened by the

Guardians of the Mersey: the fort and lighthouse on the Black Rock, New Brighton

passing of Vessels to and from the rich and flourishing Port of Liverpool, in many instances approaching so near as to admit of persons on the shore conversing with those on board.' Yet here is a prospect of wide sea views and clear horizons, with glimpses of the distant Welsh hills and, occasionally, the tops of the Lake District fells. Seabirds - waders and gulls - whirl, turn and settle on the wet sands - and, at high tide, the Irish Sea batters the sea wall, sending spray high into the air.

From the prom you can see the old coastline, a long range of low, rocky cliffs and dunes on which Atherton built his fine houses. The rocky parts which are so prominent against the green turf are known locally as the 'Red and Yellow Noses', for obvious reasons. Above the 'Noses' is a fine stretch of flowery grassland where, on warm summer days, butterflies and moths flit amongst the clovers and harebells, and rabbits hop about in the long grass.

I wonder how many of the folk who walk these pleasant airy heights realise that, a few yards below their feet, extends a labyrinth of caves and tunnels. These are the aptly-named 'Wormhole Caves' which, legend has it, extend for miles below New Brighton and Wallasey, perhaps to the site of old Mother Redcap's at Egremont, and to Wallasey parish church in the other direction. Originally a natural feature of the coast, man has, over the centuries, used and enlarged these dark caves and tunnels for his own,

sometimes illicit, purposes. If you ever get the opportunity to go down the Wormhole Caves, take it - it's quite an experience!

That last phrase sums up New Brighton quite nicely: an experience. Whether you want the peace and solitude of open seascapes and the sound of sea-birds; or the noise and clamour of amusement arcades and candy-floss stalls - the choice is yours. What more could you ask?

MORETON, MEOLS AND THE NORTH WIRRAL COAST

The lure and legends of this sandy coast facing the Irish Sea

My childhood days were spent in Moreton. I grew up within a stone's throw of the north Wirral coast, with its grassy common land behind the embankment, rich in buttercups and clovers. The sea dominated our lives in so many ways, its salty tang carried across the flat, wind-swept plains by restless breezes; the mysteries of the opposite sex being discovered in the warm, sandy nooks of the quiet dunes and, in later years, pleasures of a different kind, in the delight of discovering uncommon plants and flowers in those very same dunes.

You either love it or you hate it - this treeless expanse, these few miles of coastal plain fronting the Irish Sea. Its very open-ness disturbs many folk - there is nowhere to hide, nowhere to run, from the ceaseless wind and the frequent squally showers blown in from the sea. There are few trees - and those that survive, are bent double away from the west and the prevailing wind. And yet, there are days in summer - few enough indeed - when the warm sun shines, the skies are blue, the wind dies down for a while. These are days to be savoured: to search out rare flowers in the long meadow-grass: ragged robin, orchids, and yellow button; to laze on the soft, warm turf, listening to the skylarks singing high above, with the faint murmur of the surf on the incoming tide; or to stroll along Meols promenade, enjoying the sight of the small, colourful boats gently bobbing on the quiet tide. Delightful.

What changes this part of the Wirral coast has seen: in olden days the Irish Sea was free to pour inland across these low-lying plains, as far as Overchurch and towards Bidston. Only the concrete embankment saves these lands from inundation today. At the opposite extreme, the Wirral peninsula used to be longer than it is today; tidal waters now cover lands once inhabited by man and beast. Seek out the evidence for this in the tree-trunks and peat-beds of the submerged forest on the shore between Moreton and Meols. Six thousand years ago, these parts now covered twice daily by the Irish Sea tides, were forest lands: men hunted here, their game being red deer. Later, much later, the

Opposite: dunes and embankment protect the north Wirral coast from the inroads of the Irish Sea. Looking westwards from the site of the old Derby bathing pool towards Moreton, Meols and Hoylake, with the Welsh hills in the distance

15

Romans used this northern extremity of the Wirral peninsula as an outpost. Evidence for this, and for subsequent use by later folk, is seen in the 5,000 objects found along this part of the coast in Victorian days. Brooches, buckles, knives, tokens - they've all been found here, in their hundreds. See them in the museums, but *imagine* them in this their treasure-trove setting, here along this wave-beaten shoreline.

Much of the open space and sand dunes have been incorporated in recent years into a coastal park, with its resulting picnic tables and interpretive boards. Fine, if it helps to preserve the area. But let's not overdo it. Some places are best left undiscovered, untouched.

You can't help but discover Leasowe Lighthouse, though. It is the most prominent thing around, and dominates this stretch of Wirral coast. Long redundant, this light was an important part of the guidance system for mariners entering the port of Liverpool. Its redundancy nearly resulted in demolition not so long ago, but it now looks spruce in its new coat of paint, and with the completion of the interior refurbishment, it looks set to be an important focal point for the coastal park. Strange to say, it is once again serving the local mariners at night, when its floodlighting transforms it into a useful beacon for their comings and goings along these dark and dangerous coastal waters.

Leasowe lighthouse: sentinel against the setting sun

Leasowe light may be over 200 years old, but it gazes across the windswept grassy meadows towards something much older - and another guardian, of sorts. Leasowe Castle, grim as all good castles should be, has been here on this desolate marshy flood-plain for nigh on 400 years. Of course, bits have been added to it over the years, and its original single tower is barely discernible at the heart of the cluster of buildings that rejoice in the name of 'castle'. But the grey stone turrets are there, and it's not too difficult to imagine this as some defensive fortress to protect its founder, Ferdinand, Earl of Derby, way back when lawlessness was rife around here. They say he was involved with the popular horse-racing that went on by the sea here, and which eventually gave its name to the national Derby race of today.

I personally rejoice to see the rebirth of Leasowe Castle from the mould of dereliction and decay which beset her fifteen years ago. As you enjoy the bustle of activity around the place today, recall my words of 1981: 'As I write, the castle stands empty, derelict, as it did 300 years ago - a twentieth-century Mockbeggar . . . will these rooms and corridors ever again hear the cosy chat of people relaxing after a day's work? Will fires ever again flicker in the cold hearths? Will children ever again run up and down its staircases, discover its secret passages, run across its lawns . . . or will it continue to decay - cold, silent, with only the ghosts of times past to walk its rooms and corridors?' The answers constitute one of Wirral's greatest success stories.

Away from the coast, Moreton has grown from a small village to a sizeable community in little more than a generation, and it is still growing. Perhaps it is the air.

Leasowe Castle catches eventide rays: the grey stonework of the original building contrasts sharply with the later extensions.
In the background, Wallasey ridge and the church towers of St Hilary's

It has almost swallowed up pretty little Saughall Massie, its farms and cottages. But we are getting too far from the coast. And talking of the coast, did you know that the world's first scheduled passenger hovercraft service operated between Moreton and Rhyl in 1962? Another Wirral first. A far cry from those days, romantically portrayed by a tourist, as he walked along here earlier this century:

> 'Away out on the Dove Spit was probably situated the ancient town of Meols where, in ancient times, the Romans listened to the roar of the incoming tide, and near which their galleys tossed securely at anchor, or sped up the Dee to Chester. And so we pass on, feeling that the world is wider and older than most of us consider, and indeed a great book which, if we could but read correctly, would raise the curtains of the past and shed a new light on history.'

Romans; hovercraft; lighthouses; castles; submerged forests. Makes you think, doesn't it?

*Moreton
Parish Church*

Hoylake and west kirby

Sand, sea, skies and sunsets at the north-west corner of Wirral

Hoylake and West Kirby - the two places go hand in hand, like salt and vinegar, or Jack & Jill. But two places so close together, yet so far apart in character, it would be hard to find. In the words of a visitor about the turn of the century, 'There are those who could tell you that the two pretty places are merely on speaking terms and just painfully civil to each other. Why they differ no outsider knows. They are both endowed with good looks, they both see the daily mingling of two great rivers, and watch the same majestic sunsets; and, which is not quite beside the point, are ever ready to offer the casual stroller grateful rest.'

Perhaps it has something to do with the air - for West Kirby faces west, feeling the mild breezes which blow in from that quarter. Poor old Hoylake looks north, and gets the full brunt of polar air blowing down across the Irish Sea from the Arctic regions. Then again, West Kirby is sheltered somewhat by Grange Hill at the back, Hoylake lies open and exposed to winds from all quarters. Or perhaps the outlook plays a part in this: from West Kirby, the Hilbre Isles and Welsh hills confine the eye, giving a more homely feel,

*Opposite:
water-sports on the
marine lake at
West Kirby*

and the marine lake lends a placid foreground - Hoylake looks out across endless seas, to the far distant horizon - and lands unknown . . .

But enough of this. Let's put differences to one side and take a closer look at these two towns on this north-westerly tip of Wirral. Hoylake has no town centre, but a mile-long road of shops and an equally long promenade, running parallel to each other. It all seems very modern - which is not surprising, when you consider that before the roads and houses were built, all of this land bordering the Irish Sea coast was shifting sand and grassy dunes. Not very hospitable for early settlers! Yet Hoylake does have a past, for beyond the dunes was a deep-water anchorage, the Hoyle Lake, which was used in the 1600s as a point of departure for troops travelling with William III to Ireland and the Battle of the Boyne. What a sight that must have been for the local fishermen - 10,000 men marching down King's Gap!

Later on, Hoylake had its time as a resort - 'It is well calculated for the inhabitants of the central counties who, at no great distance from their own house, will here find genteel society, good accommodation at reasonable prices, and one of the most commodious bathing-places in the island.'

It's a fine walk along the promenade, particularly on a midsummer's evening, when they say that this is one of the few places in England where you can see the sun both rise and set over the sea. I've seen it set often enough, but have never yet been up early enough to see it rise! Looking out seawards, you'll find it hard to imagine the old deep-water

Hoylake sands: children play where sailing ships once anchored in the deep waters of the old Hoyle Lake

anchorage, when you see how much the sand has silted up in recent years. But you may spot the old lighthouse behind the promenade, which will certainly convince you of the resort's maritime past, if nothing else will!

The Royal Liverpool Golf Course separates Hoylake from West Kirby, and at the extreme tip of Wirral are the sandstone outcrops of Red Rocks. What a beautiful place this is, where the Dee estuary meets the Irish Sea: 'On this tip of Wirral the horizons are clear and wide; sky and sea predominate in a scene which is never the same for two consecutive hours. The estuary is constantly changing as tide, sun and clouds interact on this vast tract of wilderness.' Here, too, nestling amongst the sand-dunes, is a wet slack known as Red Rocks Marsh, a treasure-trove of coastal plants - orchids, star-of-Bethlehem, sea holly and wild thymes - and home of the rare natterjack toad. Here, too, the Hilbre Isles appear close-enough to cross to with ease - but it's safer to cross from West Kirby.

*   *   *

I see West Kirby as a place of strongly contrasting features, and perhaps that is the attraction of the place. Whatever your mood, whatever the time of year, there is something to do. There are, of course, the inevitable shops. But there is also the prom, with its attendant marine lake and, for those who like that sort of thing, the marine sports. (What

Sand, sea and sky meet at Red Rocks point, on the north-west tip of Wirral. In the estuary the Hilbre Isles; beyond, the low Clwydian hills and, further distant, the cloud-shrouded peaks of Snowdonia

21

a lovely walk that is, the circuit of the Marine Lake - a high-level footpath taking the pedestrian right out into the wilds of the estuary - superb!)

Those are, I suppose, the parts of West Kirby that most folk know and enjoy. But I like, too, the other, little-known parts. The old village, for example, with its ancient parish church and quaint museum, cottages and narrow lanes that twist between old walls of red sandstone overhung with shady trees. From here time-worn footpaths and ancient trackways trace their way upwards to the craggy heathland of Grange Hill and Caldy Hill. They're not high, these craggy uplands beside the Dee, but they have a magic, a charm of their own. They're wild, untamed. You have a picture here of what much of Wirral must have been like before man started to tame it. If you happen to lose yourself among the birch trees and the gorse bushes, you feel that you have strayed miles from anywhere. You start to panic. Then up looms that landmark which has served mariners for decades, and suddenly you know where you are. The Mariners' Beacon is the monument everyone knows, it is visible from all over the northern part of Wirral. There was a windmill here once, which the sailors used as a sighting line for a safe passage into the estuaries; this beacon replaces the windmill, which was destroyed in a gale in 1839 (see the old mill-stone at the base of the Beacon).

This is just the beginning of the long sandstone ridge which runs down the western side of Wirral from here to Heswall; never reaching more than about 350 feet high, but much of it open space where people are free to roam amidst the gorse, heather and bracken.

But really, most folk come to these heights for the views. And such changeless views too, for these words of a visitor about the turn of the century may well have been written

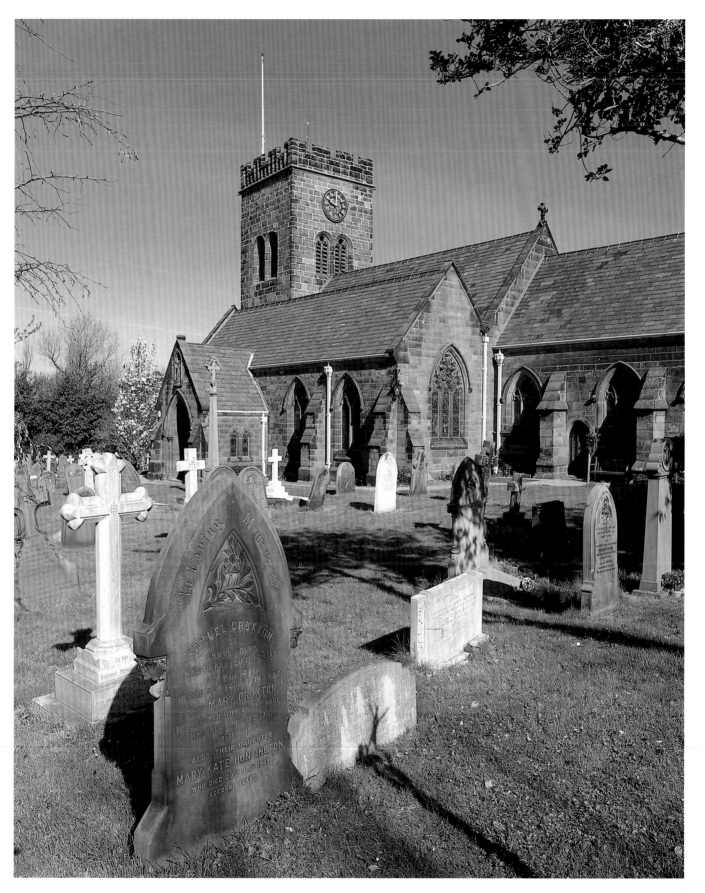

today: 'As you ascend, the horizon gradually falls away on both sides of the ridge, revealing varieties of colour and outline almost equal to the vista from Bidston Hill. On the one side rolls away the great inland plain called Newton Carr, a miniature campagna of level green areas, picturesquely marked here and there by spire, copse or hamlet. Across the water on the opposite shore Wales seems to bend forward as if loth to part with her noble river. Immediately at the foot of the hill shelters the church and village, and away beyond, Hilbre and its attendant islets are mirrored in the moveless tide. A beautiful scene at early morning, but more beautiful still when lingering sunset transfigures mountain, moor and river.'

An evening's sail at West Kirby; Hilbre Isles in the background

Opposite top: the sandstone ridge above West Kirby gives fine views of the town and the Dee estuary

Opposite below: Ashton Park, West Kirby adjoins the old railway to Hooton, now the Wirral Country Park

St Bridget's Church West Kirby

25

DEE IMAGES

A lone curlew flies across a small brook which trickles out of the
wet moorlands high in the Welsh mountains. Gathering life and force,
the brook leaps down hillsides to become a stately river, tumbling over smooth
rocks and flowing gently through quiet green meadows. At last, it leaves
behind its youth and flows, as if beckoned by some life-force, towards the sea.
Here, with Welsh lands on one bank, and Wirral lands on the other,
it broadens out into a fine and elegant estuary, a vast waste of
marsh, mudflats and sandbanks.

The river barely washes Wirral-side, with its old Dee ports and villages,
its red cliffs and its sandy beaches. But the Dee still dominates;
from our Wirral lands we see the sun set over its wide, wet reaches; we hear
its waters racing across the mudflats; and we hear a curlew calling
across the sands - the same bird that sped across this river at its birth,
high up in those Welsh Hills? Perhaps.

THE DEE ESTUARY

Wildlife and sandscapes in a beautiful surviving wilderness

I have to admit to a love affair - an affair of the heart which has been going on for nearly 20 years: half a lifetime of continuous passion which deepens as the years go by. My love for the Dee estuary is deep-rooted; when away from home I dream of, and long for, her wide, wet, tide-kissed sands, her far blue skies, her coastal reaches drenched in history, her bird life, and her tiny isles.

The beauty of this place, where the Dee ends its long journey from Welsh uplands to open sea, draws me time and again to taste its magic, its delights: on fine summer days, when the blue horizon shimmers in a haze of heat, and it is enough to lie amidst the cool bracken on Middle Eye; or in the depths of winter, when sky and sea form a continuous leaden pall, and ice crystals form at the water's edge at Red Rocks. Or those bright, turbulent days of spring and autumn when the westerly wind sweeps down from the high lands of Wales, and raggy white clouds drift across the estuary to amass over the distant Lancashire Pennines. Such days are fine times for exploring this wilderness - its wild reaches and its man-tamed edges.

Eighteen miles of the Wirral peninsula adjoin the estuary. 'From Blacon Point to Hilburee,' runs the old Cheshire saying, 'the squirrel leaps from tree to tree.' Follow the shore-line up-river today and you will find few squirrels, and even fewer trees. What you *will* find are, on the one hand, reminders of days when cargo- and passenger-laden boats tied up at busy quaysides; and, on the other, the broad mud-flats and marshes of the estuary, where the quiet lap of the tide and the haunting calls of curlew and oyster-catcher echo across the wet wilderness.

The Red Rocks form the northernmost point, an outcrop of flat sandstone from which it is possible to look eastwards along the north Wirral coast towards New Brighton and the Mersey; westwards across the wildest part of the estuary towards Point of Air on the Welsh side; and southwards up the Dee towards Chester. The Hilbre Isles are prominent, seemingly guarding the estuary from all comers, while away to the north lies the far horizon of the Irish Sea.

Following the Dee shoreline south from Red Rocks, the dunes and slacks of the nature reserve, rich in wild-life, contrast sharply with the bustle of the marine lake and promenade at West Kirby. These are soon left behind, though, and near Caldy the red cliffs of boulder-clay make their first appearance: low at first, but rising steadily towards Thurstaston and offering lovely cliff-top walks above the sandy beaches for four miles. This shore-line is lonely and uninhabited, the only abode being the white cottage nestling

*Opposite:
dramatic skies are a
fine feature of the
Dee estuary, often
changing from hour
to hour, and given
an added dimension
from the reflections
of the wet sands and
mudflats*

The White Cottage, sitting snugly beneath the shrub-clothed cliffs and facing the incoming tide by the Dee at Thurstaston

beneath the cliff on the shore at Thurstaston. No-one knows the full history of this isolated house, but it may have housed customs officers long ago, in the days when lawlessness was the name of the game along here. And for much of this century it was the home of Sally McCrae, a sprightly old lady who was the friend of local sailors and fisher-folk.

Somewhere along this stretch of coast was the old port of Dawpool, from whence Jonathan Swift sailed for Dublin - perhaps the large stones lying in the sand are all that remain of this ancient anchorage. On the cliffs, amongst the grasses and wild-flowers, crumble the ruins of old lime-kilns; and boulders from Scotland and the Lake District lie scattered about the beach, brought here by the glaciers of the last ice age.

Here too, the first tufts of marsh grass signal the advance of the marshes of the estuary, a tidal wave of green spreading relentlessly down from its upper reaches around Burton. Towards Heswall the wet mud-flats gradually give way to the marsh, and the estuary changes its character. Tidal gullies and deep pools break up the monotony of khaki green which seems to stretch to the Welsh foothills - fine in summer under blue skies, but dismal in winter when all seems grey and bleak. The Dee here has abandoned the Wirral coast, leaving high and dry the old ports which brought busy-ness and trade to Wirral folk centuries ago. Their names echo across the empty marsh: Neston, Burton, Shotwick, Parkgate. Footpaths and byways still follow the edge of the peninsula, twixt the marshland and the shore, and the solitary rambler has only the rustle of the wind in the reeds, and the cry of the birds, for company.

The birds. What is the Dee estuary, if not a place for birds? They come here in their thousands - tens of thousands - in spring and autumn. They are waders, mostly, but wildfowl too - feeding on the rich resources of the mudflats and marshes. The only thing that comes near to outnumbering them are the birdwatchers - but there is room for them all here, on this great, lonely, wild edge of Wirral.

And can we talk of the Dee estuary without a mention of Mary - that farmer's girl portrayed by Charles Kingsley, trying to bring home the cattle from off the marshes: the thickening mists, the incoming tide, the poor girl's fate out on those lonely mudflats:

'Oh Mary, go and call the cattle home,
  And call the cattle home,
  And call the cattle home,
  Across the sands of Dee'
The western wind was wild and dank with foam,
  And all alone went she.

The creeping tide came up along the sand,
  And o'er and o'er the sand,
  And round and round the sand,
  As far as eye could see.
The rolling mist came down and hid the land:
  And never home came she.

Oh is it weed or fish or floating hair,
  A tress of golden hair,
  A drowned maiden's hair,
  Above the nets at sea?
Was never salmon yet that shone so fair
  Among the stakes of Dee.

They rowed her in across the rolling foam,
  The cruel, crawling foam,
  The cruel, hungry foam,
  To her grave beside the sea;
But still the boatmen hear her call the cattle home
  Across the sands of Dee.

On those days when the pressures of everyday living overpower the heart and mind, I escape for an hour or two to these lonely byways by the Dee: alone with the sea, the sky, the birds, the distant Welsh hills, source of this lovely river, I recharge weary ways with the peace and beauty of it all. And I always return refreshed, and thankful for such a haven on my doorstep.

THE HILBRE ISLES

Precious jewels at the mouth of the Dee estuary

When I talk to people about Wirral, Hilbre usually crops up. Most folk say they want to go to these enchanting islands in the Dee estuary; but few ever actually make it. For those who *have* been, these few pages will be a reminder of happy hours; for those who have yet to go, perhaps you will be encouraged; and for those of you who cannot go, for one reason or another, join me now on a trip to the nicest place in Wirral: Hilbre.

It's a perfect day for Hilbre: we'll be staying over the tide, so the blue skies and light westerly breeze promise well for a good few hours yet. High tide's in about three-and-a-half hours, so we've adequate time to reach the islands safely. The sands of West Kirby are quiet this morning, but if the fine weather keeps up, they'll be crowded by the time we return.

It's good to be out on these wide open spaces this morning: the air is clear and the horizons are sharp. Wales looks deceptively close in these conditions, and even our own Hilbre Isles seem no more than a five-minute amble away; but as we traipse across the wet sand, it seems ages before they seem to loom closer. Behind us, the Wirral mainland gradually recedes: the buildings on the prom which recently seemed so grand are now indistinct shapes, and the tree-clad ridge of Grange and Caldy Hills are mere bumps in the distance.

Out here, all is quiet, save for the faint murmur of the incoming tide on the distant sand, and the occasional call of wading birds scooting low over the mudflats. Crossing the watery gutters and channels, we approach Little Eye, smallest of the three islands in the Hilbre group. There is little here to detain us today: a few patches of spray-washed turf, with a clump or two of white bladder campion maintaining a tenacious hold on the crumbling sandstone edges. At certain times of tide and season, every square inch of this rock is covered with wading birds resting out the high tide.

Opposite: early summer on Hilbre - pink thrift carpets the middle isle, and in the distance, beyond the rocky lagoon, Hilbre itself basks under cloudless blue skies

Turning northwards towards Middle Hilbre, we traverse a slippery, rocky plateau of contorted formations, bounded on the landward side by deep channels through which the incoming tide is starting to flow; and on the west by clean, sandy beaches beyond which we see the breakers creeping up the shore. Ahead, Middle Hilbre becomes prominent, a low silhouette against the bright sky - beckoning, enticing. At our feet, stranded on the dry sand, are a multitude of sea-things: crabs, cockles, starfish, sea-urchins and whelks. The children want to stop at every pace to poke, to collect, or to discard, each time hoping for some new rarity to claim for their own. Our own horizons

are wider, our goals more ambitious; but we do eventually scramble up the cliff-side to lie thankfully on the soft, springy turf of this jewel in the sea.

And what do we see? Unbelievable: a carpet of pink thrift covers the seaward edge of this islet. Below, the rocky bays look stark against this colourful splendour all around. We dare not walk for fear of treading it flat beneath our feet.

It is but a couple of hundred paces from one end of this small piece of tide-washed land to the other, but beyond lies a large pool, rapidly filling with sea-water, and then our goal - Hilbre itself, with its hotch-potch of buildings silhouetted against the sky.

Scrambling down the cliff-edge we reach the pool, and are soon paddling around its edge to reach the slipway to Hilbre. Our goal is achieved! We are here! And not a moment too soon, for the incoming tide has encircled the island; there is no turning back now! Around us is water, and more water, flooding up the Dee towards the marshes of Parkgate in the far distance. Now safely here, we can relax and enjoy the peace and beauty for a few hours.

The history and natural history of Hilbre has been well documented. Suffice to say that these tiny islets in the Dee estuary have been used by every generation of man down the ages. They have lived here, harboured ships here, worshipped here, worked here, played here. Last century they wanted to build docks, harbours and warehouses here - a multi-million pound commercial enterprise that would have transformed this beautiful place into another Wallasey Pool. Thank goodness that never materialised!

But despite these centuries of use, the Hilbre Isles still survive as a beautiful place for us to enjoy today. Whether we come to see the plants and birds, or the grey seals which swim around in the the deep waters, or to enjoy the far-reaching sea views; or just simply to get away from the mainland for a while, to be alone with the sky, the sea and the birds - Hilbre is always there. The most precious thing in Wirral. Long may it be so.

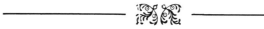

CALDY

Picturesque village lying snugly beneath a birch-clad hill

'Caldy is pretty, and the pleasure of a visit is intensified by the knowledge that it is a prettiness too assured to fear what is called improvement.' Pretty? Not a word we use much these days to describe a place, but the rambler of 75 years ago felt justified in using it. A good job he wasn't there a hundred years before, when the place was described as 'one of the worst in the neighbourhood, consisting of a few fishermen's huts and small cottages, scattered over the side and at the foot of a rocky eminence.'

So what happened to this village by the Dee to bring about such a transformation? Well, much of the credit for its change can be given to R. W. Barton, a Manchester man who came here in 1832 and set about improving the township. Of Barton's work it was

said in 1891 'It is wonderful to us who knew Wirral fifty years ago, to recognise how the master and lady of Caldy have created out of that nothing a new ideal of English home life and Christian happiness and honour.'

Today, Caldy has matured into a fine residential district. Gone, alas, are the farms; but Caldy is surrounded by natural beauty: the beach and cliffs bordering the estuary are but a stone's throw away; the heathland and birchwoods of Caldy Hill rise above the village; and the quiet gothic quality of Stapledon Wood (named after the writer and philosopher Olaf Stapledon) lies at the edge of the village. Edward Hubbard, the architect, summed it up in a fine description twenty years ago: 'By reason of its prosperous commuter country Cheshire is something of a Surrey of the north; but Surrey has nothing to compare with this.' Another local man, Norman Ellison (Nomad) summed the place up in a rather different manner: 'I ask for nothing more satisfying than a stroll before breakfast on a sunny spring morning, beneath silver birches wearing their delicate new greenery; or a brisker walk when a harvest moon is flooding the channels of the Dee with light, and borne on the still air there comes the murmur of countless sea-birds seeking their supper at the edge of the ebbing tide.'

Caldy village: the road from Montgomery Hill to West Kirby snakes through the village, where cottages of red sandstone and black-and-white timberwork nestle beneath the wooded slopes of Caldy Hill

THURSTASTON

History and beauty high above the banks of Dee

It is often said that the folk who founded our villages were looking for a warm, sheltered spot, well protected from their enemies, and with food and water supplies close by. Whoever chose Thurstaston all those centuries ago certainly found those things, but with an added bonus - a glorious view of the Dee and a panorama of the Welsh hills opposite.

The village stands proudly uplifted, nestling between the meadow-lands of Deeside and the craggy heaths of Thurstaston Common. The salt-winds sweep up from the estuary carrying the cries of gulls and oyster-catchers, to mingle here with the scent of gorse and heather off the heath-land. And, always, there is the silver thread of the distant Dee seen through the trees, through the bare branches of winter, the fiery reds of autumn, and the gossamer green of spring.

A traveller in the early years of this century described the approach to Thurstaston as he descended down from the Chester High Road: 'From above the village a steep hill overarched with trees, between whose boughs we catch a lovely glimpse of the estuary of the Dee and the Welsh Hills, leads down to the flat lands below; at its foot on the left the church, the old hall and village; on the right, a thatched cottage standing in a garden gay with flowers, and the modern Dawpool Home Farm'. Behind the cottage, a rocky bank covered with gorse, heather and broom blazes in summer; and between it and the church and hall, is spread a large green among the trees.

Most folk see little of the village as they pass through on their way to the Country Park Centre down by the shore. What a pity. The parish church dominates the Green, its ornate spire contrasting dramatically with the plain old tower of the former church alongside. What a lovely old churchyard this is! Celandines, bluebells and speedwells carpet the turf in spring, and scattered about the place are an old stone fount, sun-dial and other relics of the past. A sense of peace and timelessness pervades the air of this hallowed ground above the Dee.

All around the village you will spot references to the Ismay family - on the lychgate, on the gravestones, and on the buildings. For in this quiet little place lived, for many years, the owner of one of the greatest shipping lines ever, the White Star Line of 'Titanic' fame. Thomas Ismay brought great change to this Wirral backwater: he built a large mansion called 'Dawpool' above the village; and during his residence took steps to ensure that the tranquility of village life was maintained. Not only did he re-route the main Chester highway away from the village along its present course through the deep cutting, but he also ensured that the new railway line was routed a mile away from the

village, along the cliff-tops of the estuary. Not only that, but, finding the noise from the village school bothersome, he had it closed along with the old village inn, 'The Dog & Partridge'. Although a new school was eventually built nearer Irby, the inn was never replaced.

Whilst all this was going on, old Thurstaston Hall remained tucked snugly away amongst the trees behind the Green. Parts of this old Wirral hall may be 600 years old and, as befits such a venerable old building, it has its ghost. This is of an old woman who appeared in the bedroom of a guest one night; she was said to resemble a former owner of the hall who was supposed to have murdered a young boy - the rightful heir - to gain possession for herself. The ghost appeared in the same room in which the murder was committed.

Happily, despite some recent changes in the village, Thurstaston has not suffered as one writer suggested 100 years ago. He commented on the beauty of the place, and wrote 'A locality so favoured in America would have in no time sites marked out for public buildings, streets crowded with dwellings, with newspaper offices, churches, banks, a theatre or two, schools and other desirable institutions.'

May Thurstaston long remain free from such horrors!

The red sandstone buildings of Thurstaston catch the sun's dying rays and are seen through the green summer foliage, with a glimpse of the Dee and the Welsh hills on the skyline

The view from Thurstaston Hill - a break in the clouds sends the sun's rays to light up the lower fields and the trees of Caldy Hill. Beyond, dark cloud-banks amass over the Irish Sea to bring more rain to Wirral

THURSTASTON HILL AND ROYDEN PARK

The magic and mystery of these high lands above the Dee

'Thurstaston was always uplifted. From the beginning of time it sent all footpaths up to the ridge, and barely tolerated the Dee winding among the sandbanks below. The wise man leaves macadam far away and by field-path and woodland, by farmyard and stile, by the grass-grown byway and the glade among tall trees, he drifts across Wirral to this last playground of paths.' So wrote a visitor to Wirral just 50 years ago. He knew the magic of this high land above the Dee; this land of craggy crests, of heathy heights and leafy glades.

Thurstaston magic: I feel it in the warm wind that blows up from the Dee on spring days, as the sap rises in the silver birches to throw a gossamer green web over the woods. I feel it in the blossoming of summertime flowers on the open heath, in the sheltered glades, and in the wild hedgerows. Thurstaston magic: I feel it in the autumn mists which swirl up from the river, rear up ghost-like over the rocky ridge, and dissipate in the bronze-tinted woods beyond. And I feel it in the feather-footstep of a lone fox slinking

Late autumn frost gives a wintry feel to the beds of reed-mace in Royden Park

Opposite: the beauty of summer heathers in full bloom on Thurstaston Hill

42

through the decaying brambles on a frosty moonlit night, as an owl wings low over Thor's Stone.

Magic? Of course it's magic. There's a magic in the very name, in the very stones of this wild place high above the silvery Dee. Can there be any Wirral children - or Wirral dads for that matter - whose feet have not at some time shinned up the sides of Thor's Stone, to look proudly down on the surrounding amphitheatre as latter-day kings of the castle? Have they too not felt that magic tingle through their bodies? Even without the legends that rattle from rock to rock, this place is mysterious. We may not all believe in sacrificial offerings to heathen deities, but we all feel that quickening of the pulse, that surge of excitement, when we gaze at this awesome stone blazing blood-red in the lowering sun.

And we experience a different wonder, a different kind of awe, when we stand on the crest of the Hill, and gaze at the glorious panorama around us: the fields sweep down to the Dee immediately below, and the eye follows the estuary out to the wide, grey waters of the Irish Sea. Beyond the Dee, Welsh uplands are crystal-cut against the azure sky: Moel Fammau, and its Clwydian companions. To the north, the gentle outline of tree-clad Caldy Hill, and the outline of the north Wirral and the Lancashire coast; and out on the far horizon, the line of the Irish Sea is broken by the lumps and bumps of Lake District hills. Eastwards, the fields and woods around Irby give way to the suburbs of Birkenhead, and beyond again is the Liverpool skyline, with the faint Pennines as a backcloth. To the south, and fading into the distance, are the fields and hedgerows of rural mid-Wirral.

Somewhere amidst all this greenery the keen eye will spot the chimney-stacks of

Hill Bark, looking out over the grassy meadows and woods of Royden Park and Thurstaston Common

Opposite: flower-rich meadows bloom in a small corner of the walled garden in Royden Park

45

Hill Bark, set in the wooded grounds of Royden Park, a continuation to all extents and purposes of Thurstaston Hill. The history of this fine mansion makes fascinating reading: built on Bidston Hill in 1891 for the Royden family and removed from there lock, stock and barrel, and re-erected on its present site in 1929. Few know that another 'Hill Bark' exists: in Potsdam, Germany, built in 1913 by Crown Prince Wilhelm who was so impressed by the Wirral house that he wanted one for himself! The famous Potsdam Agreement was signed there in 1945.

Below the house, grassy meadows are a blaze of colour in summer with orchids, tormentil and bedstraw. In the woods, the smell of smoke and steam pervades the air on fine Sunday afternoons when model train enthusiasts gather to ride the rails and entertain the public. And there is a walled garden, where a rich diversity of natural habitats - ponds, wetlands, scrub, heath, woodland - can be enjoyed in a tiny area.

But perhaps all this is a bit too artificial - too unnatural. For the true atmosphere of Thurstaston can only be felt on the wild uplands of the heath, on an April evening perhaps, when the crowds have gone. The Welsh hills across the Dee are changing to purple in the gathering gloom; a pair of curlews cry across the moor below; a lone rabbit scurries into the undergrowth; and, as the chill air rises from the ground, you are surrounded by the wonder, the magic and the mysteries of Thurstaston.

IRBY

Old hall and modern shops, with a distant view of Wales

Not a stone's throw from Thurstaston, Irby too stands high above the Dee, higher even than Thurstaston: from the main village street is seen a glorious vista of green meadows rolling away, with the Welsh hills in the far distance. Here it was that the monks of St Werburgh's Abbey in Chester had their Grange, and here too is another fine old Wirral hall, protected from pillaging foes by a ditch and bank, the remains of which can still be seen. Such miscreants, if caught, may well have been locked in the nearby stocks, a replica of which stands outside the library today.

Folk who have a venturesome spirit, and a good pair of wellies, may care to search out Irby's ancient Londymere Well, down the bottom of the field-path by the Anchor Inn. This recently-discovered relic of Irby's past is most likely the well mentioned in documents dating back over 600 years. Hopefully the waters then were purer than they appear now.

Irby is surrounded by green, open space. The best is that to the north, to the high moors of Irby Heath. Here, old tracks cut across the gorse-covered heathland to Irby Mill Hill: the mill, alas, is no more, but the views across the low-lying north Wirral plain to the Irish Sea are fine. And in the nearby quarry, rock-climbers practice hand-grips and foot-holds for other, more challenging peaks.

HESWALL AND GAYTON

Old and new sit happily together on the craggy slopes of Heswall Hill

The sun rises over the Heswall ridge and catches the clods of freshly-ploughed fields above the banks of Dee

'What's the highest part of Wirral?' is a question that few folk get right. Favourite answers are 'Bidston Hill' or 'Thurstaston Hill'. Both are wrong, for the highest point on the peninsula, at about 350 feet, is at Poll Hill, Heswall. Surprising really, isn't it, for this place doesn't really feel high at all.

What other claims to fame does Heswall possess? Very few, really. It's a nice place in which to live, particularly on the west-facing slopes which overlook the Dee. The old village is a conservation area. There are some fine open spaces for walking the dog or airing the lungs. The old parish church is worth looking at. And that's about it.

But wait . . . more than any of these, but because of them - is the special, rather unique atmosphere of the place. Particularly in the old quarter. It's difficult to describe: but I think it's that happy blend of old red sandstone walls; of mellow houses and cottages, and gardens full of bushy trees and old-fashioned flowers, all sitting at random on little ledges on the rocky slopes facing the Welsh hills; of narrow, switchback-type lanes overhung with fine trees; and of occasional glimpses of the Dee and misty distant hills seen between the branches, roofs and hedges.

The River Dee drifts lazily past Heswall, where boats lie awaiting the slowly rising waters

You don't really need me to show you around Heswall: there are some excellent little village trail booklets in the local shops. But if you just had an hour to capture the best of Heswall, can I suggest the following: see the old village and parish church of St Peter, with its fine view high above the Dee marshes; walk down to the edge of the Dee, to Heswall shore, where, on a summer's evening, the boatmen are busy, and the birds - herons, waders and wildfowl - fly low over the sun-dappled channels; scramble over the Dales, a wild heathy area of gorse and bracken, and enjoy the quiet solitude of this lovely open space, a reminder of what all of Heswall was like before the houses were built; or seek out the Dungeons, a mysterious ravine where a truly babbling brook tumbles down through the woods and meadows to empty into the Dee.

An old guide-book to Wirral summed up all these things admirably: 'In a short walk one may move from the bustle of the busy streets, through quiet, homely roads, to the open country and the wide spaces where the sea-winds blow. One may choose the warm comradeship of well-lit roads with nearby shops, or the quieter homestead amid the fields, with a view of the river and the mountains beyond. Looking back to a rich past, and onwards to a promising future, the Heswall-of-the-present is a rewarding place to know.'

*   *   *

It's difficult to know where Heswall ends and Gayton begins - and really Gayton is an area rather than a village. I have always regarded the part by the Hall as the focal point

Opposite: Gayton old village, where a cobblestoned lane bordered by ivy-covered cottages leads to fine old Gayton Hall

Midsummer sunset reflected in the still waters of the channel through the marsh at Gayton

of old Gayton - it's such a charming spot, with a short cobblestoned road with ivy-covered cottages leading to the imposing entrance to Gayton Hall. What a hall! And what a history! The ancestral home of the Gleggs for centuries, this old place has offered hospitality to royalty when William III stayed here in 1689 while on his way to the Battle of the Boyne. Here too is one of two dovecots in Wirral (the other is at Puddington), octagonal in shape and dating back to 1663.

The riverbank is but a stone's-throw (or arrow-shot?) from here, down narrow lanes bedecked in spring with may-blossom and, later in the season, with wild roses and honeysuckle. Riverbank is perhaps a misnomer, for the Dee passes near the Welsh side, unseen across the endless marshes. The old ferry cottage still remains at the marsh's edge, a reminder of the days, long gone, when folk from all around the Dee side of Wirral, and from Wales too, converged on Gayton for the annual Wakes:

> Up rose the sun, the sky was clear,
> And gently ebbed the Dee;
> The winds of heaven were fast asleep.
> Though Gayton all was glee.
>
> From Hoylake Hall to Gayton came
> Fine ladies - gentlemen
> They come, my friends, to look at you
> And you may look at them.

And what an occasion that was: 'As the visitors arrive, the side-shows spring into life with all kinds of wonderful entertainments. There is a man who eats glass bottles and stones; a dancing-bear; human oddities of all kinds - giants and dwarfs, fat ladies and thin men. The place resounds to the playing of pipers and fiddlers. There are races and competitions for the more energetic: ducking for apples in a barrel of ale; a sack-jumping match; catching a pig by its tail; grinning through a horse-collar.'

And, way up on the sandstone ridge above Gayton, the sails of the old mill would have been spinning steadily around. The mill still survives, sail-less now, but its tower preserved in a housing development. That, perhaps, sums up Gayton and Heswall - the old and the new living more or less happily with one another; and long may they continue to do so!

PARKGATE

The past splendour of an old port gazing across the Dee marshes

'All on one side - like Parkgate' runs the old Cheshire saying, signifying the raw end of a deal. And raw deals were to be had in plenty in old Parkgate, particularly for those unfortunate enough to be left waiting for wind and tide to be right for their vessel to leave for Ireland! Picture the scene about 1750, wintertime; a nor-westerly gale has been blowing steadily for days. Travellers from the south, fearing Welsh terrors in the mountain passes en route for Holyhead have opted to sail from Parkgate instead. The Irish-bound vessels lie straining at anchor out in the Dee, tossed and torn by the merciless winds blowing in from the Irish Sea.

On shore the passengers, amongst them perhaps Dean Swift or John Wesley, while-away the long hours, snug and well-entertained in the cosy Wirral inns, but spending both time and money which could no doubt be better used elsewhere. Not that the Parkgate innkeepers worry too much about that! Other folk - local lassies perhaps, with loved ones amongst the crews - pace their mean cottages anxiously, awaiting news of boats long overdue from Dublin.

At last, the skies clear, the seas subside, the wind drops a little and comes round from the south; and suddenly all is hustle and bustle on the quayside. The Irish boat will leave at noon!

Such times seem so remote now, with one-sided Parkgate facing westwards across the greensward of marshes which seem as immeasurable as the sea itself; a rushy carpet unfurling to the very foothills of Wales. Can this be the same place to which folk flocked from near and far to delight in the resort's facilities for the newly-found pastime of sea-bathing. Fine golden sands, health-giving breezes, magnificent views, lured those who could afford to idle away hours in this way. From all over the north and midlands they came, to sample Parkgate's delights. A traveller described the scene at Parkgate on a fine summer's day in 1813:

Overleaf:
'All on one side' lies
Parkgate, seen here
from the marsh
which put an end to
its days as a port

'At high water there is a general burst of business and animation. We arrived at just such a juncture, when the beach was all alive, and discovered a spectacle which a foreigner might have moralised upon with more seriousness than we of this free country can be permitted to do. Few of either sex thought it necessary to hide themselves under the awnings of bathing machines: posts with ropes fastened to them are fixed in the sands, and these were taken possession of by numerous groups of women, six or seven in a row, jumping, shouting, laughing and screaming, evidently as careless of being seen as of being drowned.'

I wonder . . . what did the local fisher-folk, those who made a meagre living from the dangerous, swirling waters of the Dee, think of it all? Did they ignore it? Were they slightly envious? Or did they, perhaps, make a pretty penny or two themselves during these decades of plenty pouring into the place?

Today, the sea has gone, the travellers have gone, the sea-bathers have gone, the fisher-folk have gone. So what is left? There must be something, for every fine afternoon, winter and summer, brings nose-to-tail parking along the front. People walk from one end of the long Parade to the other - for what? I know exactly what they come for - because I do the same myself, many times a year. We come, not to study the detail of the hotch-potch of old buildings along the front; nor to examine the finer points of history which surround Parkgate. No, we come here to feel the fresh west wind blowing on our faces from across the desolate marsh; we come to capture that unique feeling that only Parkgate can give - a slightly surreal landscape of wide skies, marsh, and hills; we come, too, to gaze across the marshes; we come to recapture that sense of history that we know is written along this short mile of quayside. And in our mind's eye, what do we see? 'Ghosts of sailing ships leaving for Ireland? Bathing-machines with their occupants coyly splashing about in the water? A young boy swimming across the swirling channels to the Welsh coast? Fishing boats returning, low in the water with their day's catch? All of these, perhaps . . . and yet none.'

But let's not ignore the buildings, the old inns and entertainment houses which were so prominent in Parkgate's past, and whose histories are well documented in the little guide books on sale in the local shops. Consider how welcoming this little cluster of houses and inns must have appeared to the sea-weary travellers approaching Parkgate 250 years ago after a long and hazardous sea voyage. Buy the famed Parkgate ice-cream, nibble the Parkgate shrimps, and - *enjoy* Parkgate as those travellers of old enjoyed Parkgate too!

Opposite: the endless marsh, intersected by wet gullies and brackish pools, is the dominant feature of the Dee shore along this part of the Wirral coast. In the middle distance, the old colliery jetty; and in the far distance, the tree-covered headland of Burton Point

54

Neston and ness

Busy village, quiet walks and a lovely garden beside the Dee

'The wayfarer who finds himself in Neston will, given time and desire, discover more than one or two interesting nooks in this old Wirral town.' That was 75 years ago; but those 'interesting nooks' are still there, to be sought out by those with the 'time and desire' to do so. Don't let the hustle and bustle of the town's central shopping area put you off. There is much more to Neston than shops and the busy High Street: seek out the fine old parish church with its ancient stones; and the old inns and buildings in the narrow ways and backwaters. Each has its own history, a tale to tell - perhaps of the days when Neston was much frequented by the travellers using the nearby port of Parkgate.

It's unlikely that such travellers would have been terribly impressed by Neston, for in those days it attained this very unflattering description: 'The flatness of the country and the prevalence of sea breezes, which prevent the growth of timber, have given the parish a very naked and cheerless appearance; much of the land is very bad, with miserable roads, without a single tree to shelter the passenger from the severity of the winds.' Sea breezes? It seems rather far-fetched today to think of Neston as a maritime town, but it's not too far from the town centre to the edge of the Dee. They built a quay here - more of a jetty or pier, really - 400 years ago. A big project, for small returns, for hardly had it been completed than the silting-up of the Dee made it a white elephant (or red herring?). But the new quay brought trade, and prosperity, to Neston, making it for many decades the most important town in Wirral.

When you've had enough of seeing the town, stroll down to the Dee coast: it's a lovely walk across the meadows from the church, and good to feel the wide open spaces again. This is a fascinating place, full of character. There's the endless marsh, of course; and the ever-present Welsh hills. You'll stumble across old stone sea defences by the old quay site; and, not far away, a slag heap. Coal? Here in Wirral? Yes - poor quality stuff mined from under the Dee from the 1750s to the 1920s. You'll see photos of the last miners to work here, in the nearby Harp Inn. This old hostelry gazes across the dreary marsh to Wales now, but in olden times it looked out upon storm-tossed waters, and no doubt many's the time the sea-water has swirled around the front parlour. Nearby, you'll see the old stone jetty used by the coal sloops serving the colliery.

What a sad, lonely place is this part of the Dee coast, so different from the busy scenes when the mines were working and the boats were busy at the quays: 'Here once was arduous life and the clamour of commerce; now, except for the rustle of hidden wings in the undergrowth, or the soft echo of a distant shotgun, nothing breaks the brooding silence.'

*Opposite:
lovely Ness Gardens,
a happy combination
of plants, trees and
water*

The little village of Ness looks unremarkable enough. Just a couple of red-stone farm buildings and cottages along the winding road between Neston and Burton. Yet in this tiny place, 'one of the most miserable in the Hundred', was born, 200 years ago, a baby destined to shake the roots of Society. Daughter of a poor Ness blacksmith, she grew up to become one of the beauties of her generation, a natural actress, a talented singer, friend of politicians, theme of poets and painters, her name associated with scandal and gossip. Her name? Emma Lyon, later to become Lady Hamilton. That she was the lover and mistress of Admiral Lord Nelson was no secret. She stood at his side in public, in the face of all her critics.

I wonder what the humble folk of Ness thought of it all? They who had seen this little child, so innocent, and of such lowly station, in her cradle in Swan Cottage? Emma, Lady Hamilton, mistress of Lord Nelson. Born in poverty in Ness, Wirral, April 1765. Died a pauper in Calais, France, 1815.

Ness, of course, has another, more widely-known string to its bow: Ness Gardens. Facing west on the warm, sunny slopes above the Dee, this is one of Wirral's most popular attractions. And it seems to get better as the years go by! Here you will find rare and exotic plants from all over the globe: from Europe and the Americas, from China and Japan. All, apparently, thriving in our mild Wirral climate. Amazing. But then, everything to do with Neston seems amazing.

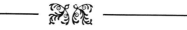

BURTON

Quaint cottages and flowery gardens line the old village street

Burton churchyard on a summer's evening: swallows and house-martins skim low over the time-worn headstones; a weary rambler rests thankfully in the lush grass in the shade of the old square tower; children's voices echo from deep within the adjacent woods; and time itself seems to carry no meaning in the musky, dusky air of this ancient place. Burton slumbers on.

But it was not always so. Four hundred years ago the village boasted five licensed alehouses (there are none now!) scattered along the main street. These were busy days for Burton, with trading vessels anchoring in the shelter of the rocky headland down by the Dee, and goods of every description being brought ashore for conveyance to Chester. Small wonder then that the parish church is dedicated to St Nicholas, patron saint of both mariners and moneylenders! There were probably plenty of both in medieval Burton.

There are reminders of Burton's past in every nook and cranny of the village. The cottages perched high on the outcropping sandstone along the main street testify to antiquity; search out the birthplace and home of Bishop Wilson, one-time Bishop of the

Opposite: the parish church of St Nicholas, Burton, with its one-finger clock and peaceful churchyard of time-worn headstones; behind the church, a footpath through Burton woods brings the walker to the legendary Quakers' Graves

Isle of Man and benefactor to Burton; consider the many building styles and materials used in the cottages; and admire the quiet beauty of the old-fashioned flower gardens.

Look out too for other reminders of how our ancestors lived: sit by the still waters of Hampston's Well in a small dingle below the village; climb through the woods to the hill-top behind the church, and find the crumbling stones and timbers of the old mill; or sadly reflect upon the religious intolerance of the past when you gaze upon the two Quakers' graves beside the footpath through the woods - Burton folk buried outside consecrated ground for their religious nonconformity.

The Dee is unseen, but not too distant from Burton village. The river wends a wayward course beyond the extensive marsh - several thousand acres tended by the RSPB as a nature reserve. Here, now high and dry but once visited twice daily by the waters of the Irish Sea, stood the ancient hospital of Denwall. Founded in the Dark Ages ' for the poor applicants of Ireland and others', there is nothing left now but a few lumps and bumps in the fields down by the marsh.

A little further up-river is Burton Point, a rocky headland once washed by the sea but now facing the Welsh coast across the featureless marsh. Dykes traverse in all directions, keeping out the sea of yore from the Wirral coast, but now redundant, unless of course the sea levels rise again . . .

From here we look back towards the village, lying snugly beneath its tree-clad hill, peaceful, serene. I recall the words of another visitor to this place about the turn of the

Like most of Burton's cottages, Barn End sits happily and securely on a sandstone outcrop, its front garden bedecked with old fashioned flowers

century, and nod assent to his comments: 'Burton, ever beautiful, is a place to linger in towards evening. Except the softened ring of the anvil towards the end of the village, not a sound comes from the shaded street. Beyond the marshes there is no murmur from the sleeping tide. The complaining note of the wood quest dies in the leafy thickness. Twilight has found you a haunt of ancient peace'.

Peaceful Puddington, where the road from Burton twists through the village and around the tiny green

PUDDINGTON

A quiet place with a rich history

Puddington Lane, an inviting-looking byway shaded by overhanging trees leads off Burton's main street, to meander for half a mile between meadows high above the Dee marshes. Puddington was described many years ago as a tiny street of 'queer roofs, red steps, grey walls and green branches. There is no inn, no shoeing forge, no noise, and the only sign of life is now and again a faint flutter round the cottage post office.' Now even the post office has gone, so what is there left to say about the place?

Indeed, very little. It is certainly picturesque, in a homely sort of way. But really its interest lies in its past. For this was the Cheshire seat of one of the greatest of the old fighting families of the county, the Masseys. Throughout the middle ages no body of Cheshire archers was complete without a Massey of Puddington, and in most of the battles of the French wars we find at least one of the family present.

The Masseys lived at Puddington Old Hall, once described as 'that gallant, lofty seat overlooking the sea'. The Hall still stands, and what tales it could tell of its colourful past. Particularly of William Massey, a staunch Jacobite who joined the Pretender's forces at Preston in 1715 but fled for home after the surrender to the Royalists. William, astride his favourite horse, rode without slacking rein until he reached Speke Hall on the Lancashire side of the Mersey. From here he swam across the river, which in places was 2 fathoms deep and 3 miles across, to land on the Wirral bank near Hooton. From there he headed for Puddington, having ridden for over 45 miles without a break, and that at the ripe age of almost 60! Alas, his faithful horse dropped dead in the courtyard of the Hall, and William was later arrested and thrown into the dungeon at Chester Castle, where he died. He was buried at nearby Burton.

The only other feature of interest here is the dove-cot or columbarium, one of only two in Wirral, the other being at Gayton Hall. So let's leave Puddington to its peace, with the words of a rambler of long ago echoing in our ears: 'Beyond the marshes of emerald sedge and the great river arise the mountains. Puddington is singularly quiet; it is so quiet that it has never yet reached the fame of a picture postcard. A place in which it would be a sacrilege to hear a gramophone.'

An old Wirral cottage

SHOTWICK

The silent village overlooking the old course of the Dee

'Shotwick Village only' declares the road-sign beside the busy Welsh Road, pointing down an inviting hedge-banked country lane which twists and turns through the lush pasture-lands of this southernmost extremity of Wirral. About the turn of the century it was even prettier: 'Here the primrose still stars the banks, here are the cowslips, celandine, milkmaid, speedwell, and other humble country flowers more beautiful to

Cottages, farms and
church line the
lonely street of
silent Shotwick

the true lover of the country than the rarest exotics; the greed of man has not yet roughly torn the jewels from the bosom of mother earth to pawn them for a few pence in a suburb; here is the music of the countryside, the murmur of the brook, the soft cooing of the pigeons and the droning of the bee.'

The lane ends at silent Shotwick, a rewarding surprise for those who take the trouble to seek it out - a cluster of old Cheshire cottages watched over by the solid-looking red sandstone church. You will find here no inn, no village store or post-office: only the TV aerials remind us that we are in the twentieth century. What you *will* find, in the stones of the buildings and in the pattern of the surrounding countryside, is a record of the past, a past which is one of the most colourful in the peninsula and which belies the peace and tranquility of this wonderful place.

A stroll past the church down the cobble-stoned lane sets the scene: during Roman times, perhaps even earlier, Cheshire salt was carried into Wales along this 'Saltesway', which was later used as the 'King's Highway' to lead ' the host of our Sovreign Lord the King in time of War unto Shotwick Ford'. Henry III and Edward I used this track and its ford over the Dee to lead their armies into Wales during the warring years of the 13th century; and despite the hazards of shifting sands, wayward channels and unpredictable tides, peacetime travellers preferred this to the more circuitous route into Wales.

Mellow brickwork, cobbled pavements and tiny iron-framed windows typify this ancient village

But this tale of tides, shifting sands and channels seems far removed from the scene before us today - a far-reaching, flat landscape of green fields backed by the hills of Wales. Can this Shotwick be the same place that once boasted a harbour, a safe anchorage where merchant and warrior fleets lay at anchor? Yes, for Shotwick was long ago perched right on the coast-line of the Dee; only a field's-length from the church the clay cliffs were twice daily washed by the tide. The steep, grass-covered cliff-line remains today, stranded by thousands of acres of silted-up pasture land; and the old creek to the south of the church still conjures up images of boats at anchor. The waters of the Dee, alas, visit Shotwick's shores no more.

The church, though, remains: well worth a visit to view the fine Norman doorway and three-decker pulpit, age-darkened box pews and many other fascinating features to be expected in a building of such antiquity (can you see the deep grooves in the porch where the Wirral archers sharpened their arrows?). 'But what are mere words when describing such an ancient, holy building as this? Words alone cannot convey autumn sunlight filtering through coloured glass and tinting the rough-hewn stone walls; or the wooden box-pews dark with age; or the cold, grey stone floor trodden by centuries of worshippers' feet. Sitting alone in the church, one's mind seeks and searches for answers to questions: What kind of people worshipped here? And what role did the church play in Shotwick's history?'

Stroll through this quiet village, admire the characteristic old Cheshire cottages with their old-fashioned gardens; seek out the old hall. Savour the peace and tranquility today, but in your imagination picture the scene from Shotwick's busy past: 'The great barons assembled here with their retinues, the street ringing to the tramp of armed men marching with warlike bustle, and in the mornings the famous Wirral archers at practice with their longbows'. Savour all this and be thankful that, despite the reminders of industrial Welsh Deeside in the far-off distance, Shotwick remains unique, untouched - and silent.

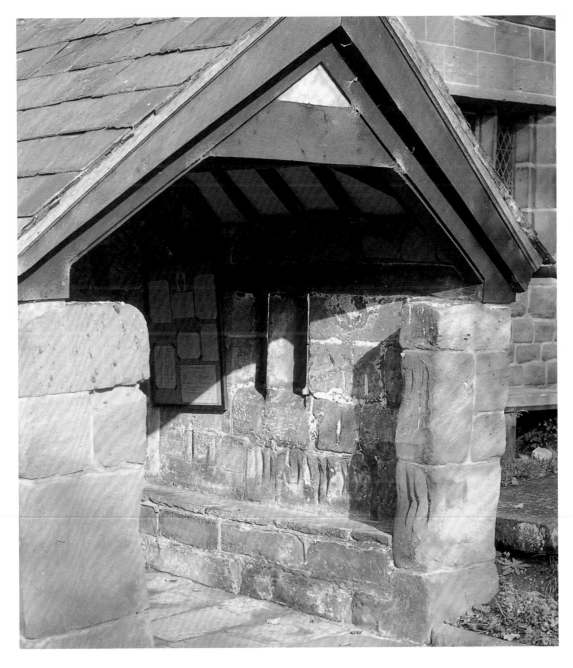

Shotwick church porch:
note the
legendary grooves
made by the
Wirral archers

MERSEY IMAGES

*The gulls scream and dance above the foaming wake of the little ferry-boat as
it sails across the grey waters of this great river.
From the top deck of the boat can be seen almost the whole of the
Wirral bank of the Mersey, from New Brighton down past Birkenhead and
beyond Bromborough towards Eastham.
Commerce commands the scene; and that is right, for this river was tamed for
trade, and on trade it developed and grew to world stature and dominion.
The docks, public buildings and houses which line the riverbank for
over a dozen miles, each have a story to tell; just a small part of the
many images which are part and parcel of the River Mersey.*

THE RIVER MERSEY

Life-blood of Wirral's eastern bank

The 'Mountwood' ferry-boat slips away from Woodside across the calm Mersey waters for Liverpool on the opposite bank

The Western Gateway, they used to call it. This great river which dominates Wirral's eastern edge was the life-blood to all who lived and worked here. Her influence extended far beyond her granite banks: this was a symbol of Empire, her murky waters taking and fetching wealth from the four corners of the globe. This wealth helped shape Wirral as we know it today, for good or bad. These briny waters which wash Wirral's shores have been both a barrier and a life-giving artery to our peninsula. A barrier which has, over the centuries, kept Wirral separate from the port upon which so many have been dependent for their livelihood; and an artery without which Wirral might have remained a poor northern backwater.

To me, the Mersey has always existed. I cannot recall a time when it has not been part of my awareness. As a child I played upon Seacombe's sandy beaches, conscious even then of the pulsating rhythms of the mighty waters breaking on the rocks below. My school-years were spent within sight, sound and smell of the River Mersey: dank,

grey November mists drifted up from the river to permeate our equally grey playground and classrooms. The tuneless notes of music lessons were accompanied on such days by the similarly cheerless wails of foghorns sounding across the river. On January days of howling gales we would daringly dodge the mighty waves splashing high over the promenade wall down by old Mother Redcap's, to return after lunch-hour with our school uniforms drenched with tainted Mersey brine.

Later years brought the excitement of New Brighton - the attractions of fairground and tower, and of romantic strolls along the prom on dusky summer evenings, arm-in-arm with the girl of the moment. Even then the Mersey predominated: silver moonlight and the pin-point lights of Liverpool reflecting off the placid, lake-like waters, ruffled only by the occasional crossing of a ferry-boat. Far out towards the Bar, the channel lights flashed intermittently, the Bar light itself shining over all.

And now the river is, to me, still a mighty thing. Whether sailing across its waters on the ferry-boats, passing idle hours on its grassy banks at Eastham, or briskly walking its promenades at Wallasey, the Mersey still rates highly in my images of Wirral.

I love the ferries. Not many left now, alas, compared with years ago. The old landing-places make a long list: New Brighton, Egremont, Poulton, Seacombe, Woodside, Monks', Birkenhead, Tranmere, Rock, New, and Eastham. Some have ancient origins, and the hazards of the primitive river-crossing are well described by travellers such as Celia Fiennes who crossed the estuary in 1698 and stated that it was 'hazardous to strangers to sail in the winter . . . it is of great breadth and at low water is so deep and salt as the sea . . . the waves toss and the rocks great all round it as dangerous as the sea'. A

The Liverpool skyline, dominated by the two cathedrals, seen from the esplanade at New Ferry

far cry from the comfort and convenience of today's Mersey crossing, which is a delightful experience at all times and in all seasons.

It's from the ferry-boats that we get the best impressions of our Wirral bank: man-made all the way up to Eastham, where the trees overhang the rocky low cliffs. Difficult to visualise how it looked 200 years ago, when the coast about Wallasey was described as being 'sandy and barren, and the only trees that existed grew close to the mouth of the river near the shore. There was scarcely a house between the Rock and Wallasey'.

As I read those words I think of the changes now taking place along these Wirral shores: the regeneration of old docklands into marinas and leisure centres. I think too of the effects a barrage might have across this great river that has flowed uninterrupted to the sea for millennia. In a brief span of only 200 years the Mersey edge of our peninsula has changed almost beyond recognition.

Yet still the river ebbs and flows twice a day; still its waters - daily growing cleaner - wash Wirral's shores: today, gently, silently; tomorrow, hurtling and crashing before violent seas. 'The flow of these tides always continues. As now, so in prehistoric times: long, long before these floating-stages, these docks and far-converging ships, long before these iron piers ran out from the Cheshire shore - before, and long, long after them was, and shall ever be, this restless Mersey.'

WALLASEY

A town of villages with a fascinating history

What a difficult place to describe - it's not really a town, for a town usually has a definable centre or focal point. It's obviously not a village, either. A suburb? - how unglamorous a word for a place with such a rich history as this! For Wallasey is really a collection of outgrown villages which have become one residential area over a period of time.

Being born and having spent my schooldays in Wallasey I admit to a certain fondness for the place. I never knew, of course, the Wallasey of old - a place of country lanes and old thatched cottages, of flowery crofts and grassy pastures, of sandy wastes and rocky heights. The old villages of Poulton, Seacombe and Wallasey are no more - only their faded images on old picture-postcards remain to remind us of the manner of life here in former times. But let's potter around and see what there is of interest in Wallasey today.

Wallasey's highest point, the Breck, is a good place to start. From this elevated, gorse-covered wasteland on which was perched the old Wallasey mill, one gets the lie of the land. Westwards across the low-lying Moss lands towards the wooded slopes of

Evening sunshine catches the long sandstone ridge of Wallasey, with the twin towers of St Hilary's church dominating the skyline

Bidston Hill with its windmill, and beyond the distant Welsh hills. Further round towards Leasowe with its sand-dunes and a glimpse of the waters of the Irish Sea. In the other direction, the quiet docks on Wallasey Pool, once a wet, swampy arm of the Mersey which in bygone times connected with the Irish Sea on the north Wirral coast.

The ridge extends northwards to come down by Harrison Drive, that fine, open area of old sand-dunes right by the sea. Midway along here stands the parish church of St Hilary, proudly overlooking the old village which she has served for nearly 1,000 years. This church's legendary links with the smuggling which was carried on hereabouts are well known, one tale being that when the church caught fire, the blaze from the liquor hidden within could be seen for miles around! It is also said that underground passages link St Hilary's with the site of Old Mother Redcap's at Egremont, a popular haunt of the smuggling fraternity in olden times. Scattered about the churchyard are inscribed gravestones - sad reminders of the violent shipwrecks which were a feature of this wild coast. Sad to say, some Wirral folk of those dark days were hardly the good samaritans one might hope for:

Vale Park: a summer Sunday afternoon by the bandstand. Through the trees, a glimpse of the Mersey

'On stormy days and nights, crowds might have been seen hurrying to the shore with carts, barrows, horses, asses or oxen even, which were made to draw timber, bales, boxes, or anything that the raging waters might have cast up. Many a half-drowned sailor has had a knock on the sconce whilst trying to obtain a footing, that

Wallasey's town hall is a landmark along the Wirral bank of the Mersey

has sent him reeling back into the seething water, and many a house had been suddenly replenished with eatables and drinkables and furniture and garniture, where previously bare walls and wretched accommodation only were visible. Then for smuggling: the fishermen used to pretend to cast their nets to take the fish that abounded on our coasts, but their fishing was of a very different kind.'

It seems a far cry from shipwrecks of old to the busy shopping centres of today. Liscard could be any shopping place in the kingdom, but this was once open, common land stretching down to the Mersey; the wife of one of the owners of Liscard Hall, in Central Park, was able to see her husband crossing the river in the ferry-boat!

Down by the Mersey, Egremont and Seacombe are riverside places with fine views across the river to Liverpool. Recent work here has achieved superb results, with low- and high-level riverside walks overlooking one of the most interesting commercial estuaries in the country. It seems a far cry, though from the days when the people of Seacombe 'opened their windows to let in the west wind which blew freshly over the fields, bringing some of the sweetness of the heather and gorse on Bidston. They sat there evening after evening, to watch day's golden death and, when the sun sank and all the land was still, there was the distant friendly gleam from the light in the old lighthouse.'

One of my favourite parts of Wallasey is the area around Vale Park and the

Magazines. Here, right by the river, was the storehouse for Liverpool's gunpowder and, nearby, lovely Vale Park, with its domed bandstand and memories of childhood days listening to punch-and-judy and other summer delights.

Of the tales behind the old inns and buildings I have little room to relate; the interested reader will have to search elsewhere for these and other anecdotes. But I do have room to restate my fondness for this corner of our peninsula which, despite the houses, roads and shops, contains a wealth of interest and delights, and friendly atmosphere, and always, 'the tang of ozone in the air to invigorate the tired spirit'.

BIRKENHEAD

'The City of the Future' with a wealth of interest

They used to bathe, ride donkeys, and gather periwinkles on Birkenhead beach in the olden days. That was a long time ago, of course - when meadow-lands swept down from the heights of Claughton Common, Oxton and Tranmere to the banks of the Mersey: banks so unlike the granite-and-iron of the present day. The Birkenhead edge of the Mersey was a tumble of rocky headlands clothed in greenery: high tides lapped against ferns and wild-flowers, and birch-branches dipped leaves and twigs into briny waters. Birches? Headlands? Of course - Birkenhead! Hard to picture it today, though. The hotels, the beaches, the greenery - it's all gone. Swept away when Laird built his shipbuilding yards here 150 years ago. That, really, was the end of the birchen heads, and the beginning of Birkenhead.

You'll perhaps get a glimpse of what it may have been like here all those years ago, in quiet corners of the old Priory. You'll have to find a spot where the tall ship-repairing cranes are out of sight, for they intrude somewhat. There are a couple of shady nooks though; gloomy corners amongst the hallowed, ancient, time-worn stones, where gentle autumn sunlight dapples the greensward. In such corners you may imagine you hear the monks singing vespers; in the background, the cry of sheep on distant pastures; and the lapping of the clear Mersey waters on the beach below the Priory. And glimpse, perhaps, the ghosts of medieval travellers awaiting safe passage across what was to become one of the great commercial rivers of the world.

Pioneering. That's the word that springs to mind when I think of Birkenhead. The great river which touches this town's edge sent many folk westwards across the Atlantic, to start new lives in new lands, thousands of miles away. But they were equally pioneers, who came only half-a-mile across the turbulent Mersey waters, or from across the Irish Sea, to settle in Birkenhead and found this new place. They came with nothing but a vision of a better future for themselves and their families; and they carved roads,

railways and buildings on these green Mersey banks . . . 'One of the facts which have most deeply impressed us lately is the sudden rise of a new city in England. We allude to Birkenhead on the Mersey . . . one of the greatest wonders of the age . . . the grandest monument which the nineteenth century has erected to the genius of Commerce and Peace.' Prophetic words indeed!

Pioneers? Of course - they created here in Wirral England's first public park, the first tramway service, the first public library. You name it, and it was probably first thought up in Birkenhead. This place had everything going for it. It should have arisen to become one of Europe's most important, most beautiful cities.

But it didn't. Perhaps it is too close to Liverpool - the younger brother syndrome? Birkenhead never got a chance to develop its own personality. It gave a shrug, even turned its back to the river - shut it out from its people. A riverside town, with barely a glimpse of its life-force. Final report: 'Could have tried harder.' But enough negatives. Promote the positive side.

Wonderful waterfront - and getting better all the time. Have you ever seen sunrise over the Liverpool skyline on autumn mornings, with the little ferry-boats scuttling across the gold-crested waters to Liverpool? Magnificent. Same word applies to Hamilton Square: the formality of its buildings beautifully matched by the symmetry of its

The fine gardens of Birkenhead's Hamilton Square are dominated by the grand town hall and complemented by elegant office buildings

75

The Boathouse in Birkenhead Park sits elegantly beside the Lower Lake, basking in the early morning sunlight of a bright summer's day

neat lawns and colourful flower-beds. A real study in Victorian splendour and four-square Victorian values. In contrast, Birkenhead Park's great attraction is its very unpredictability. What a superb blend of woodland and water, grassland and gardens. And odd buildings - boathouse, bridge, lodges - glimpsed through the greenery of beech branches and rhododendron bushes.

Then those lovely Victorian suburbs - so majestic, so solid, so permanent - and so green, so unexpectedly leafy. Particularly the higher parts - towards Oxton, with its attractive narrow lanes and old sandstone walls. Almost a feel of the countryside here, in summer, when the little gardens are bright with rich-hued flowers. Other high places adjoin Birkenhead too - Prenton, its older, leafy parts especially nice (famed for its wood mentioned in Doomsday); and Noctorum, with grand views west across north Wirral towards the misty Welsh hills.

This all seems far removed from those riverside places down by the old Priory, where it all started. Those old stones, so rudely awakened from their slumbers by the coming of commerce a century and a half ago - they've seen the fortunes of man rise and fade, as the wind on the Mersey and the very tide itself. What, I wonder, will be the fate of this City of the Future as it goes into the Third Millennium?

St Andrew's Church Bebington

BEBINGTON AND ROCK FERRY

From Mersey banks to breezy heights

'Bebington - the very name visualises a quaintly-winding street of irregular roofs, leading up to broad tree-shaded roads, and rising clear above the branches is the soaring spire of the old church'. That was way back at the turn of the century. The soaring spire is still there but the quaintness, sadly, has gone. Bebington is now a pleasant place in which to live, with few reminders of the past. It's sandwiched between the Mersey and the mid-Wirral countryside, with part of it low-lying, and part extending up towards the Storeton ridge.

The Mersey bit, embracing New Ferry and Rock Ferry, is a place of contrasts: from the Victorian grandeur and eloquence of Rock Park to the mean streets adjoining the old

Opposite top: the Boathouse interior, Birkenhead Park: admire the recently renovated ornate floor

Opposite below: dappled summer sunlight relieves the sombre shadows and gloomy corners in Birkenhead Priory, perched high on the river-bank above the River Mersey

Chester road. What is nice, though, are the occasional glimpses of the River Mersey seen between the houses. Nathaniel Hawthorne, who stayed here as American Ambassador to Liverpool 150 years ago, was not so endeared to the river, which he thought would be 'a pleasanter object, if it were blue and transparent, instead of such a mud-puddly hue'; sentiments shared by everyone today. Yet there are occasions when, under blue skies and placid conditions, this broad, almost lake-like part of the river does indeed seem blue and transparent. Walk along the old esplanade on such a day, and see what I mean.

Bebington's a place for puzzlers. If you like a mental challenge, have a go at working out the answers to the riddles on the famous puzzle-stones in the Mayer Park, in the village. The old, odd eccentric Thomas Francis carved these, and others, over 150 years ago, for the amusement and entertainment of idlers and passers-by. His pranks and

When the people of Bebington murmured for want of water, I cut the rock and God gave them plenty
Thomas Francis

Opposite:
a surviving corner of
leafy Rock Park:
Victorian splendour
with a view of the
Mersey

eccentricities are still talked about in Bebington today. And mention of the Mayer Park reminds me of another Bebington personage, the philanthropist Joseph Mayer, a Liverpool merchant who gave the village a free library, a museum and, of course, the Park.

St Andrew's parish church sits quietly in a leafy backwater of the village - 'one of the finest old churches in Wirral', with Saxon foundations. But listen - if you are worried

about problems such as the end-times of the world and doomsday, then take a quick peek at the ivy climbing the church-tower. A legendary prophecy suggests that when the ivy at Bebington reaches the top of the spire, then the end of the world will be nigh. We've little to worry about for a good few years yet - on my last visit I could find only a small piece twineing around the base of the tower!

Higher Bebington covers rising ground towards Storeton ridge. Men have taken this fine-quality stone since Roman times for building purposes. You'll see the scars of quarrying all around Storeton hill, and many of the older buildings were connected with the workings and their associated tramways. Here, too, were found fossilised footprints of the dinosaur Cheirotherium, left in the wet sands millions of years ago and preserved in this sedimentary rock until exposed by quarrymen 150 years ago. They can be seen now in the Williamson Art Gallery in Birkenhead.

Most folk come here nowadays to stroll through the pleasant woods which cloak the hill. These are really quite beautiful, at all times and in all seasons. I like them particularly in late autumn, when the golden tints of the fading leaves shine brightly in the light of the sun as it lowers over the distant Welsh hills.

It is said that the old Cheshire prophet, Robert Nixon, once came to Storeton hill. Whilst sitting here, admiring the view no doubt, a local miller asked him where a man might find safety on the Day of Judgement (was he worried about the ivy on Bebington church, I wonder?). Nixon replied: 'In God's Croft, twixt the Mersey and the Dee', evidently referring to the Wirral peninsula; but why he thought that Wirral should be any more blessed than elsewhere is hard to say!

The wishing gate
Higher Bebington

Up here too was the famous Wishing Gate, where lovers and courting couples came in the quiet evenings to plight their troth. One old resident recalled that they stood, one on each side of the gate, then solemnly shook hands through the bars and kissed each other over the top. Many of the couples, too, left their initials carved into the gate, an enduring testimonial to their avowed love for each other.

From these wooded heights, green pastures stretch westwards as far as the eye can see, dimly intersected by neatly-cropped hedges and dotted with small copses and ponds. You can see little, if anything, of the Mersey to the east; but something of the character of this wild ridge as it was 150 years ago can be seen in the following description given by Albert Smith in his novel *Christopher Tadpole*: 'They had gone for some little distance over broken ground, encumbered with huge blocks of stone, and dug

Willow Cottage sits snugly in a leafy corner of Lower Bebington, a surviving reminder of former, more tranquil days

into deep quarries and pits . . . but Christopher's attention was principally attracted by a swarm of lights that he was looking down upon on his right, the like of which he had never before witnessed. They rose, bright and twinkling, even in the last gleam of day, one above the other, until the most distant and the faintest appeared to mingle with the peeping stars that one by one were coming out in the blue air. Their reflection gleamed and quivered in a great water that flowed between them and the headland.'

Nathaniel Hawthorne's home Rock Park

TO OUR
GLORIOUS
DEAD

ACTON A.C.
ADAMS A.M. M.C.&BAR
ALDERWOOD A.
ALLMAN I.W.J.
ALLWORK
ANSELL C.E.
ANSELL H.J.
ANYON
ASPINALL G.
ATKINSON
ATKINSON

BENSON
BENSON
BENYON
BERGOT
BIRCH F.W.
BLACOE
BLAKE

PORT SUNLIGHT

Factories, cottages and rose gardens by the Mersey

The banks of the Mersey have few enough attractions for the seeker of the picturesque, with its factories and commercial activities; yet it is upon such enterprises that one of the most attractive spots in this part of Wirral was founded. 'How often we who love the country find rural beauty destroyed by manufactures, land bare and barren, sky dulled by smoke; look at yonder village, clean and neat; look at those roads lined with young elms and chestnuts, at the half-timbered Cheshire cottages each with its garden plot, at the stone bridge, the little church, the fine halls and the immense works. Port Sunlight is a lasting honour to the men who own it and built it.' That was written in 1903, when the village was barely complete; no doubt the writer would go into raptures over the place today, after a century of maturity.

I go to Port Sunlight on those days in May when the blossom-trees are in full flower and the gardens are ablaze with wallflowers and tulips. It's too early in the year for the roses - that is a mid-summer treat to look forward to with anticipation. But the village on such days looks new, fresh and clean. Sunshine and shadow highlight the ornate detail of the houses, throwing the fine plasterwork into sharp relief. W. H. Lever's dream of building houses in which his work-people could 'live and be comfortable - with gardens back and front' - in which they would be able to 'know more about the science of life than they can in a back slum, and in which they will learn that there is more in life than the mere going to and returning from work' - has been fulfilled here at Port Sunlight.

On such days as this it is difficult to imagine this Mersey bank before Lever cut the first sod - most of it being just a few feet above high water and liable at any time to be flooded by high tides, becoming virtually indistinguishable from the muddy shores of the Mersey. Today, as the sunlight dapples through the ornamental trees in the grassy Dell, can we believe that this was a branch of the Mersey, filled with ooze and slime, and sending forth malodorous stenches?

Go, visit Port Sunlight. Pick up a leaflet from the Heritage Centre and spend time admiring the cottages and public buildings, the gardens and open spaces. Spend an afternoon in the Art Gallery, built by Lever in memory of his wife: wander around the elegant rooms, study the work of the great painters, admire the craftsmanship of the fine furniture, and marvel at the discerning taste of Lever himself, who assembled this beautiful collection. 'And come often, for each time you will discover a new pleasure, some detail previously unnoticed, such is the richness of this collection.'

Coming out of the subdued light of the gallery into the warm sunshine outside, with

Opposite: the War Memorial stands guard over the wide, green boulevard which forms an impressive approach to the Lady Lever Art Gallery, seen in the distance

A group of cottages which typify the unique village of Port Sunlight

the fine, wide boulevard leading the eye to the war memorial in the far distance, one is struck by the congruity of the whole. Nothing jars the eye or the ear. It *is* possible for man to create harmony out of chaos; the world of commerce need not be ugly, dirty and noisy. Port Sunlight is a living testimonial to one man's vision of a better world, of better homes for the people. Let the final words be his: 'In homes the most precious products in all the universe are created - the bodies and minds of human beings. Everything that enters into a home manifests itself sooner or later in the bodies and brains of men and women. The wrong kind of home means the wrong kind of people and the wrong kind of citizens.'

BROMBOROUGH, POULTON AND SPITAL

A fascinating area of rich history and quiet beauty

Opposite: a lovely corner of Brotherton Park, Bromborough

One thousand years ago Bromborough was the most important place in Wirral, with a weekly market and an annual fair attracting folk from all over the peninsula to buy and sell, to work and play, to entertain and be entertained. Victorian writers described

Bromborough as 'an ancient, respectable village' and 'owing to its natural beauty and proximity to Liverpool, it has become a favourite place of residence'. The weekly market has, sadly, long gone - but all the other adjectives still apply.

I have many, mixed images of Bromborough - on the one hand fine, modern, residential areas; and on the other the quiet wooded river-vales of Dibbinsdale. I see a cluster of commerce about the Pool, and more modern factories along the Mersey bank; and in my mind I also see St Patrick landing here from Ireland 1,500 years ago and blessing a holy well in a shady corner of the village. I see the old market cross and parish church in the heart of the village; and I see the Saxons fighting the Norse forces at the battle of Brunanburgh, here on the banks of the Mersey, a millennium ago.

The Pool, of course, is an arm of the Mersey; an estuary on an estuary. Today its outer reaches are used by industry, but inland it twists and turns and grows narrower towards Bromborough Bridge, where it was described 200 years ago: 'The adjacent rocks and woods, a watermill, and a serpentine current of fresh water, make a beautiful landscape.' Where the Pool empties into the Mersey is a unique and little-known Wirral village. This is not an old village in the usual sense of the word, but as a planned, 'model' village it actually pre-dates Port Sunlight. Prices Patent Candle Company built 'Bromborough Garden Village' in the 1850s for its factory workers. It was a self-contained community; which was just as well, for its isolation was the subject of the following comment: 'Birkenhead was five miles away and Chester thirteen, and before the 1914 war it was not unusual for men and women to walk to one of those towns and back again. But most people stayed at home in rural peace. It was a static corner of England: one man slept for 58 years in the same bed in the same cottage'.

I stand today in the centre of Bromborough village, by the old market cross, and reflect on those words. Around me cars and buses hurry here and there; folk dash in and out of shops and supermarkets. How times have changed. Oh for the peaceful days of old. It is refreshing to enter the sanctuary of the church grounds, a quiet, hallowed acre amidst this busy place. I study the old Saxon stones, and wonder what stories they could tell: of bloody battles and deadly conflicts . . . did I say 'peaceful days'? . . .

*　　　*　　　*

'Situated in the southeastern part of the township, at the back of a deep and richly-wooded dingle, Spital presents a scene of sequestered beauty . . .' That was in 1847, and little has changed. Oh yes, some new houses have been built at the Bebington end, but the wooded part around Poulton Hall remains unspoilt, much as it may have been a thousand years ago when the Lancelyns built a defensive castle here as their homestead which, standing on a high knoll, overhanging a deep vale in front, and flanked by two ravines, was remarkably strong.

The castle has long disappeared, but the descendants of this long-established Wirral family still live here at Poulton. The seventeenth-century hall of the Lancelyn-Greens sits proudly looking out across this lovely part of the peninsula, over woods and meadows, to the far-distant Welsh hills. In this quiet corner of Wirral has lived generation after

generation of a family which, although in many ways unremarkable, has each added a little to the quality of life down the ages. We talk glibly today about 'heritage' - this is real heritage, these few beautiful acres of land and buildings, so carefully looked-after down the centuries. Long may they continue.

A lone heron stands gracefully in the brook which runs through Brotherton Park

*E*ASTHAM VILLAGE

Old cottages and wayside inns in a leafy setting

'Eastham is the finest old English village I have seen, with many antique houses, and with altogether a rural and picturesque aspect . . . there were thatched stone cottages intermixed with houses of a better kind . . . it was not merely one long wide street, but there were several crooked ways, gathering the whole settlement into a pretty small compass.'

Nathaniel Hawthorne wrote those words almost 150 years ago. At the time he was

the American Consul to Liverpool, but living in Wirral, and this is but one of many word-portraits he painted of these villages dotted about the Mersey bank.

I have a certain fondness for Eastham akin to Hawthorne's. I'm not sure why: its rural aspect has all but gone, and its proximity to the busy Chester road taints its atmosphere somewhat with noise and dust. Yet it still has that village feeling about the place. It is leafy, there are few modern-day intrusions and, in the stillness of a spring morning Eastham could be in the heart of rural England.

Folk pass through Eastham on their way to the Ferry and Country Park. A few of them stop off to search out the fascinating history behind the buildings we see today. Even fewer track down the oldest living thing in Wirral; they find it in the corner of the churchyard - a venerable yew tree. How old is it, everyone asks. Perhaps 1,500 years old, says the plaque affixed to the tree. The next question is usually: Is it the oldest in England? Wirral folk say it is - others say not. Whatever, despite the gaping hollow down the middle of the tree, this specimen looks set to live on for another millenium yet!

There's quite a lot else to see in Eastham besides the yew tree; take a guided tour of the church, for a start. Yes - Eastham sets a sparkling example of showing off its heritage by offering visitors a guided tour of one of the finest old parish churches in the peninsula. If only other parishes might do the same! Then look at the old cottages and inns - and imagine Eastham as it was in the days when two dozen or more stage-coaches a day passed through en route to the Ferry, bringing passengers to the Liverpool boats from Chester and beyond.

Hawthorne gave us a lovely glimpse of the homely way of life inside one of Eastham's inns in those times: 'There was a cheerful fire in the grate, a straw carpet on the floor, a mahogany sideboard, and a mahogany table in the middle of the room; and on the walls portraits of mine host and his wife and daughters - a very nice parlour, and looking like what I might have found in a country tavern at home, only this was an ancient house, and there is nothing at home like the glimpse from the window of the church and its red ivy-grown tower. I ordered some lunch, being waited on by the girl, who was neat, intelligent, and comely, and more respectful than a New England maid.'

Eastham is close enough to the River Mersey to occasionally have the salt-tang of the sea in the air, when the breeze blows up from the east. On such occasions it is easier to visualise the days when Eastham's fortunes were more closely tied to the river - when her folk eked out livings from the tide's flooding and ebbing, either as fisher-folk landing their catch, or as boatmen and innkeepers whose livelihood depended on the wayfarers who passed through the village.

They, of course, have long since gone; but the river remains, passing by this ancient village as if it did not exist. Let's go down the Ferry Road and take a look at it.

Opposite:
Eastham parish
church with its
unusual broached
spire and famous
yew tree

Eastham country park

Trees and meadows fringe the racing Mersey waters

A wooded waterside. What a happy blend of nature's elements: a place where bark and branches, briars and beeches meet the tidal waters of a great river; where ancient trees cling precariously to craggy cliffs, and leaf-dappled sunlight catches foam-crested waves.

I first saw Eastham Ferry on a magical day in late April, many years ago. We had traipsed through Bromborough and were glad to leave the noisy Chester road and enter the quiet sanctuary of these old woods around Eastham. It was a springtime wonderland of nature's rebirth: a misty green haze of unfurling leaves above a groundsward of wood-sorrel and freshly-opening bluebells. Woodland birds rejoiced all around at the warming air, the welcome sunshine, and the excitement of the mating season.

Then, a new scent amongst the perfumes of wild-flowers and springtime greenery: the salty tang of Mersey brine carried up from the river on the slight breeze. Wirral folk recognise that scent well: it speaks of eternal voyages across endless oceans to far-off lands. It permeates our coastal edges at certain times of wind and tide, and reminds us of our maritime heritage, of our close ties with these waters which lap the shores of our peninsula. So, that April day, we were ready for the unfolding view through the budding twigs, of our great river running past the old stones of Eastham. Ready, but still enchanted. We, who had only ever seen the Mersey waters from concrete promenades, were enthralled by the natural beauty - yes, beauty - of this place by the water's edge.

If that was all there is to Eastham Ferry, it would be enough. But it has more - much more: a fascinating history, the evidence for which can still be searched out in the woods and by the river. This is an ancient place. Folk have been carried across to the Lancashire shore from here for hundreds of years: a hazardous and risky journey, by all accounts, one Victorian traveller being 'much terrified by the appearance of the water'.

Opposite: the lovely wooded cliff-line at Eastham Country Park; in the foreground, the remains of Job's Ferry, and in the distance, a tanker emerging from the Manchester Ship Canal at Eastham Locks

This place reeks of the past: a short walk along the cliff-top reveals ancient sand-stone blocks and time- and tide-worn steps cut into the riverbank - remains of old landing-places. And in the adjoining woods, hidden amongst the rhododendrons, more remnants - Victorian fountains, monkey cages, a bear pit, ornamental walks - all remind-ers that, a hundred years ago, this was the mecca, on fine summer Sundays, for those with money and leisure time. Paddle-steamers brought them over from the Lancashire side to walk through the shady arbours, to be entertained by exotic animals and performing humans. They sat beneath the fine trees, and by the cool fountains, sipping refreshing teas; with one eye on the weather, no doubt, hoping for a calm journey home! Not all trips ended in golden sunsets: 'And now it is time to go on board the ferry boat again. The

white gulls have settled in flocks on the sand banks in the middle of the estuary . . . gradually the sun is becoming obscured by cloud; a chill wind is coming up from the sea, driving the passengers from the upper deck . . .'

One hundred years on from those merry days of leisure-trips and picnic parties, has much changed? Perhaps not. We don't call them Pleasure Grounds now, but Country Parks. Same thing, new name. People still flock here on fine afternoons, not by boat, but by car. They eat and drink here, enjoy the views, walk through the woods, sit and relax, romp and play. The only things missing are the bears and the boats. Bring those back and perhaps, as a visitor said 150 years ago, 'Eastham - the Richmond of Cheshire, as it has not infelicitously been called - will rival the glories of its former popularity'. Perhaps.

*E*LLESMERE PORT

Nature and commerce along Wirral's southern edge

Some of my favourite bits of Wirral lie in this nook of the peninsula which the map-makers and town planners call Ellesmere Port. No - not the civic centre, the shops, the industrial areas or the housing estates. Nor even the Boat Museum, fine though that may be. The bits I like best are those that man has tampered with the least - the quiet, lonely places of woodland, river and meadow where the birds sing and the wild-flowers bloom. In such places it is possible to discover remnants of what this area may have been like before commerce took over, pushing out most of the old and beautiful, and replacing it with the modern and, often, ugly.

Like Wallasey, Ellesmere Port is a name used to cover lots of smaller places which have grown to become one larger entity. Village names still remind us of the scattered, agricultural and riverside communities which have been lost in recent times: Whitby, Netherpool, Overpool, Little and Great Sutton. Old guidebooks offer nostalgic glimpses of a way of life gone for ever: 'The village of Overpool, embosomed in hayricks and branches, heavy with ripening fruit'; 'Little disturbs the peace of Little Sutton except the clank of milk-cans in some paved dairy-yard, the querulous murmur of drowsy poultry, or the snip of the shears in some cottage hedgerow'. Change had to come, of course, once the canal was built. A port is a port - a place of business, activity and growth. But not just one canal came: this place boasts two canals, both designed for different purposes, but both having a dramatic effect on the growth of Ellesmere Port. All this is vividly portrayed in the Boat Museum - that tremendous achievement which has turned a run-down industrial eyesore into one of the foremost waterway experiences in the land.

What is it about running water which attracts us? When visiting the Boat Museum, I always feel the urge to leave the static exhibits and exhibition halls, and follow the Ellesmere Canal as it disappears beneath the quaint little bridges into the mysterious

*Opposite:
the Boat Museum at
Ellesmere Port:
something for
everyone*

beyond. I love this walk along the towpath - from industrial heritage, through modern-day petro-chemical plants, and into the charming Cheshire countryside, where Wirral truly ends. Canalside villages - Little Stanney, Stoak and Croughton - add interest to the walk, and with the lovely city of Chester as a destination, what could be nicer?

Water of a different kind makes another of my favourite places around Ellesmere Port: a little brook running through grassy meadows sloping up to wooded heights. Rivacre. Another country park for Wirral. Country park? What a dreadful name for an enchanting place of bluebell woods and meadowsweet glades; of springtime drifts of celandine and summer shows of campion and foxglove. Of warm, grassy, sunlit meadows where butterflies flit from flower to flower; where dragonfly-wings sparkle above the silent pools in the summer sunshine.

This part of Wirral has other hidden delights: Church Wood, Childer Thornton; and Stanney Wood. Even the Wirral bank of the Manchester Ship Canal is a fascinating place: overhung by trees and branches, squirrels scamper by the waterside, and the peace is occasionally disturbed by the gentle throb of a boat pushing its way towards Eastham locks and the open river.

High summer along the river-bank in Rivacre Valley Country Park

My last favourite bit of Ellesmere Port is also to do with water: ancient Stanlow, a place of hallowed ground. An island off a peninsula, a green, rocky place facing the desolate Mersey marshes and mudflats, and separated from mainland Wirral by the Manchester Ship Canal. Here, where the curlew and oyster-catcher utter their eerie cries,

lie the crumbling stones of an old abbey, overshadowed by the gleaming aluminium pipelines of oil refineries. In winter, icy winds and damp Mersey mists swirl about these ruins to penetrate the marrow and chap the skin raw. No wonder the monks fled to Whalley in the end.

A traveller returning from Stanlow 75 years ago summed it up admirably: 'As we move quietly away to the boat, to be rowed across the ship canal, the buried past, in which we have been dwelling, and in fancy almost hear the great bell calling the faithful to evensong from across the marshes, is suddenly forgotten, as a steamer hurries swiftly along the canal on its voyage through eastern Wirral to the great ocean beyond, and spells for us the great change that has occurred in our habits, thought and lives, since the good Cistercian monks held sway at Stanlow'.

Ellesmere Port: alongside the Manchester Ship Canal. In the distance, Mount Manisty, an artificial hill constructed from the spoil produced when the canal was dug out

VILLAGE & COUNTRY IMAGES

The golden sun rises slowly above dew-soaked pastures,
while a gentle breeze rustles the branches into wakefulness as another day
dawns across the Wirral countryside.
A flock of rooks drifts noisily across the cloud-flecked sky towards
fresh feeding grounds on the other side of the peninsula.
In the villages, life stirs; the farm workers take to the fields; and the
commuters head for the towns. Milk floats and delivery vans
break the peace of the quiet lanes which criss-cross this patchwork quilt of
countryside; and, with the approach of day, the lone fox slinks back
into the safety of the dark copse by the mere.
These are just a few of the images which make up the beauty and interest of
Wirral's countryside.

BIDSTON VILLAGE AND HILL

The beauty and interest of old-world village and heather-clad heights

'It was a little, quiet, grey village - so very grey indeed, and venerable, and quaint, that no flaunting red brick had dared to show itself and break the uniform tint of its gabled antiquity.' Grey - yes, that's a good word to describe Bidston. And the other adjectives which Albert Smith used 150 years ago still apply too - little, quiet, venerable, quaint. But its greyness overpowers - everything about Bidston is grey, even on a bright summer's day. It's to do with the stone, of course, from which everything in the village is constructed - walls, cottages, old hall, church - all quarried from the local sandstone from the long ridge which begins here at Bidston and ends down Bebington way.

I suppose every local person over forty holds a sentimental image of the Bidston they knew before it was swallowed up by the march of time. With the adventure-land of the hill rearing up behind, it was the mecca for summer days out for families from the towns of Wallasey and Birkenhead. The smell of the countryside pervaded the air from the moment the train pulled in at the station - the reed-beds of Bidston Moss extending away towards Wallasey hill; the squat, grey tower of Bidston church nestling amongst the trees; and may-blossom lanes leading enticingly up towards picnic-meadows and bluebell woods.

The hill, of course, is still a lovely place. And the village? Well, let's see. The cottages, hall and church still survive as they ever did, and are probably in better condition now than for many years. You can still stare at the old Ring O'Bells Inn and imagine its oversized host, Simon the Cellarer, preparing his famed ham and eggs for the crowds at holiday weekends ('on such occasions the inn yard would be crowded with gigs, spring-carts and traps of every description'). Or wonder at the architectural fascination of Church Farm, with its 13 different floor levels. You can consider the aloofness of Bidston Old Hall, reposing high on its sandstone shelf above the village and once the home of the Stanleys who played an important part in the Civil War.

Yet there is something sad, something rather wistful about Bidston. Perhaps it is the knowledge that its days as a country village are truly over; or perhaps it is the memories of carefree childhood days that can never be regained; or perhaps it is just its greyness, exuding from the very fabric of the place.

*   *   *

If it was only for its quiet pathways through heath and bracken, extensive views across the northern part of the peninsula, and cool walks through shady woods, then Bidston

Opposite: Bidston Mill, well-known landmark all over the northern part of Wirral, and centre of attraction for all who scale the craggy heights of Bidston Hill

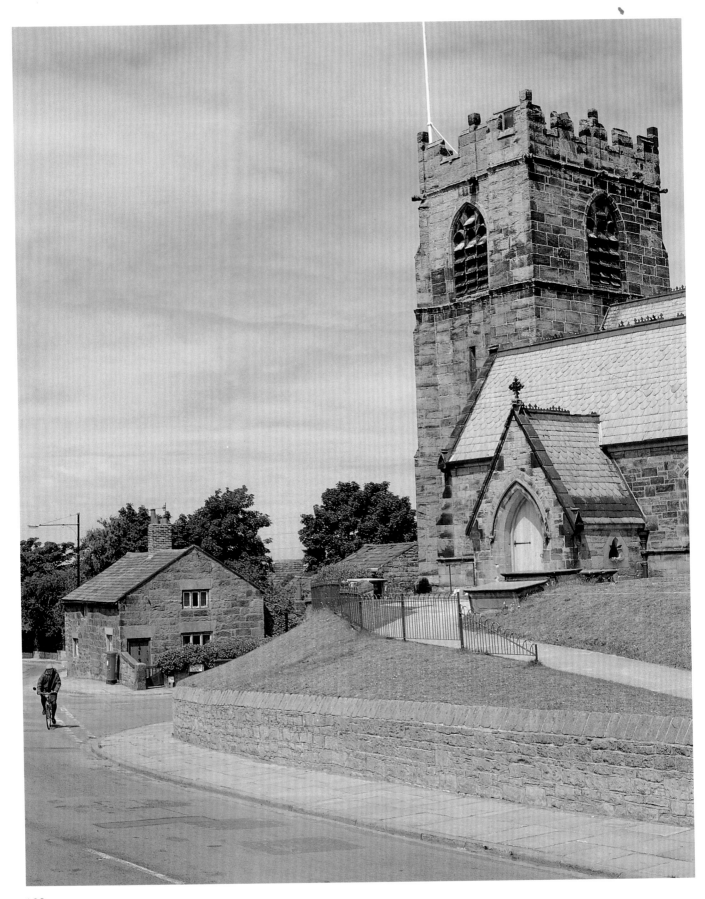

Hill would be a delight. But add to these an old windmill, an observatory, a lighthouse, all with a rich and varied history, and you have on these breezy upland heights an exciting and fascinating treasure-chest of interest.

To the children of Wirral, this has always been a wonderland. Their earliest memories are of summer picnics on the springy turf, of heather-picking on golden August days, of climbing the gnarled oaks scattered about the craggy slopes, and of spying through the tiny keyhole in the old mill's door, seeing shrouded shapes in the dusty darkness.

Bidston mill has always been a prominent feature of the skyline, dominating the wooded ridge for miles around. It's the last of several mills that have stood here over the centuries, and must have been a grand sight in the days when the eternal breezes up here spun the great sails. Today, of course, the mill's internal workings are no longer a mystery, for folk can view the old cogs and gearwheels on one of the mill's many open days.

This long ridge has other delights too: the old observatory (now the Institute of Oceanographic Sciences) with its twin domes; and the lighthouse, a reminder of the days when the navigation of shipping into the Mersey estuary relied on candle-power and sight-lines rather than electronic gadgetry. Other relics of the port's golden maritime days can be seen in the rows of post-holes set along the ridge, where the semaphore signal flags were erected to warn shipowners of their ships' imminent homecoming.

Scattered about the hill a keen eye will spot images cut into the soft, grey rocks of the hill: a sun goddess with outstretched arms; a life-sized horse; and countless names and initials of folk long forgotten. Hidden in the undergrowth too are the remains of an old cock-pit, a reminder of the somewhat inhumane pastimes in which country folk indulged.

A few crofters' cottages lie scattered about the hill's lower slopes, the most famous being Tam O'Shanter's cottage, complete with carved gable stone illustrating Tam's drunken exploits. Now delightfully restored as a field study centre, this old place was almost razed to the ground a few years back.

Bidston Hall

But for many folk, the attraction of Bidston hill is the open ridge and the fine views which it commands over this part of Wirral. Perhaps it is best to tell you how a visitor saw the view from here 150 years ago, so that you can compare it with the view today: 'The lover of the rural and picturesque is struck with the burst of scenery which presents itself . . . the hamlets of Woodchurch and Upton, in sequestered beauty, amidst verdant pastures, waving corn, and masses of foliage on an undulating surface . . . Wallasey,

*Opposite:
a corner of grey
Bidston. The parish
church dominates,
while below is the
old Ring o'Bells Inn,
where Simon Croft
served up his famous
ham and eggs in
olden times*

Leasowe Castle and Lighthouse, with the low land along the margin of the sea sweeping to the estuary of the Dee . . . with Moel Nant and the mountain scenery which flanks the eastern side of the vale of Clwyd . . . in front when the weather is favourable, appear the Great and Little Ormesheads and Penman Mawr . . . while to the southward are the magnificent Carnyds, and alpine scenery to the peaks of Snowdon and the sugar-loaf crest of Moel Siabod . . . and distant churches and villages, beautiful and verdant enclosures, together with the placid ocean and every description of vessels in the distance.'

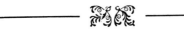

UPTON, ARROWE AND WOODCHURCH

New communities, ancient villages, and fine Victorian parkland

'A level, green country spreads out before you . . . here and there along the dark ridge, trees are set like lace against a marigold sky . . . the wide pastures rich in the varying greens of the meadows and woods make a swift appeal to town-tired eyes . . . this Wirral vista is never more beautiful than in its cool green raiment of early June.' That was how Woodchurch and Arrowe appeared to a traveller coming down Prenton hill from Birkenhead 75 years ago. Changes there have been in Wirral, but the transformation of this once-rural area to the suburbia of today must be one of the most dramatic of recent years. These little villages of outer Birkenhead slumbered on peacefully for much of this century, unworried by the spreading tentacles of the town 'over the hill'. Now we must look hard for the few open spaces which still remain amidst the dwellings and the shops.

Upton, of course, was for long an important meeting-place for the villagers of north Wirral, its weekly markets and biannual fairs drawing folk from near and far. From the village hill the scenery was enlivened by 'the distant prospect of the sea and the numerous vessels trading to and from the port of Liverpool.' And talking of shipping, we must remember that the founder of the famous Inman Line, William Inman, lived in Upton Manor in Victorian days. Inman, described as 'a strong Conservative and a man of no ordinary ability', was responsible for the introduction of screw-steamship passenger emigration to America.

Almost opposite Inman's manor house, and hidden amongst the undergrowth, is the ancient site of Overchurch, a strange and wonderful place lost in the heart of suburbia. Here was founded, 1,000 years ago, a church and settlement, in those days right on the edge of the shore. Old moss-covered headstones remain, lying at crazy angles in the undergrowth; and here, too was the Overchurch Runic Stone, described as one of the oldest inscribed stones in the north of England - 'The people raised this

Cricket on the green: a summer match at Upton Cricket Club

memorial - pray for Aethelmund'. . . See this mysterious memorial stone in the Williamson Museum, or a replica in Upton Parish Church.

*　　　*　　　*

It's a pity it is called a 'Park', for today that conjures up visions of formal flower-beds and neatly-trimmed privets, of golf and bowls. Oh yes, Arrowe Park does have those things, but to me the real Arrowe Park is a rather wild place - a green oasis of flowery meadows, and woods full of bird-song. It is a place to search out clumps of primrose and violets in early spring, and regal orchids later in the summer. It is a place to follow the tortuous course of the Arrowe Brook in search of a kingfisher, or to lie beneath lofty beeches watching the antics of grey squirrels.

The Arrowe estate was laid out around the Hall in the 1830s by John Ralph Shaw, a wealthy Liverpool warehouse owner and a keen huntsman. He it was who planted the fine woodlands we enjoy today, and dammed up the Arrowe Brook to form the lovely lake and waterfall at the western edge of the Park.

The Park knew international fame for two glorious, muddy weeks in July 1929 when it hosted the Scouts' World Jamboree, an experience still remembered and talked about by those who attended the event. Over 50,000 scouts converged on Arrowe from all over the world during one of the wettest summer spells this century. The Jamboree became the Mudboree, with special raised walkways being erected over the worst-affected areas. However, spirits remained high, and it was stated that much of the Jamboree's success was because of the spirit of comradeship generated by the awful conditions!

Although sadly built upon for the hospital on its eastern side, the Park is still a lovely oasis amidst the bricks and mortar of this part of Wirral. I leave you with the words of a visitor here some years ago: 'From the wide crest of Arrowe Hall Park you command a view of most of the peninsula. Hall and hamlet rise here and there in the stretches of green corn, the sullen moor is lit with torches of yellow gorse. In the high elms the rooks are wrangling in their airy city, and now and then on the wind comes the long wailing of the Irish Sea,'

*Woodchurch
Parish Church*

Very few folk who go to Arrowe Park ever take the trouble to cross over the main road to visit Woodchurch. Which is a pity. If you think of Woodchurch only in terms of housing estates, can I encourage you to visit the remnants of the old village, by the church. It's possibly the earliest Christian church site in Wirral, and has features which make it a fascinating place to look over. Come here on a sunny day in spring or summer, sit in the shade of the ancient church tower, and you will soon forget that Woodchurch's fields are no more. Slumber awhile as the breeze rustles the branches of the fine old trees about you, and picture this place as it was in times past - a farming community whose living depended on the produce of the surrounding land - folk whose lives, hopes and fears were confined to this small nucleus of cottages, church, and fields. And look at the community that lives here now - people still with hopes and fears - but based now on a wider view of life - way beyond the old village bounds - people with a world-view of life - and are they any happier than those folk of old Woodchurch. I wonder.

*Opposite:
Anglers enjoy a few
summer hours
away from it all
on the lake in
Arrowe Park*

GREASBY

A new community in a rural setting

'Inconveniently situated, at some distance from the ferries, in a remarkably poor and cold country . . . the land is inferior, the rocks in many parts rising to the surface.' Recognise it? That was Greasby 150 years ago. What, I wonder, would Mortimer say today of this place of smart new housing estates and sophisticated wining-and-dining establishments?

Not all of Greasby's past has been swept away, though. Small remnants exist, in odd corners of the village. Visit the old water-pump, focal point of village life throughout the ages, and lovingly restored a few years ago as a reminder of an important part of our heritage. See also the village cross, an iron structure at the side of the road to Irby Hill - agricultural labourers would gather here in olden times to be taken on by local farmers to work on the land.

Most of the old farm buildings have been 'done up' almost beyond recognition, and are now eating-houses or inns. The old hall still survives, looking somewhat out-of-place amidst the new brick and gleaming ironwork of modern-day Greasby.

FRANKBY

Old farm buildings and houses set around the village green

Frankby, too, is undergoing change. There are no housing estates yet, thankfully, but the old farm buildings are being turned into living accommodation. This old place still boasts a village green, but its old charm is somewhat spoilt by the busy road which twists through the village. It's worthwhile seeking out Frankby Hall, in a commanding position at the top of the nearby cemetery. This fine mansion was built in 1846 by Sir Thomas Royden, and is now a chapel and office for the surrounding estate.

But Frankby is a good place for rambles, with lanes and footpaths leading the walker to the lovely heathlands of Thurstaston and Irby Hill. One such walker left this image of the area about the turn of the century: 'The pathway here winds over land as flat as any in the Fens, but it runs in deep rich grass and beautifully close to the sheltered hedgerows from which every light breeze just now shakes down snowdrifts of falling blossom. In the spinneys the cuckoo note still rings joyously. Down amongst the dyke flowers, bees are busy at their plunder, and in a few days the rambler will be led along by the odour of new-mown hay'.

LANDICAN

A quiet place with a sense of history

From these Wirral villages footpaths lead the rambler to the heathlands of Irby Hill and Thurstaston Common

I like Landican - the village, that is. Village? - hardly. Just a couple of farms and cottages on a twisty bend on a quiet lane. Truly rural, yet within a stone's throw of the motorway and the housing estates of outer Birkenhead. This place is old - ancient even. Was there an early church here ('Lan' seems remarkably like 'Llan', the Welsh word for church)? There is no other evidence for one. Yet Landican is supposed to have been more populous and of greater value than any township in the Wirral Hundred except Eastham.

I love its isolation, and its field-paths which lead to other lovely Wirral villages - Storeton and Barnston. In the words of a visitor 80 years ago: 'Here at least is picturesque isolation. It is very small and very old. Seemingly a place without history, and yet not unknown to fear and bloodshed. Tradition has it that a headsman of the sixteenth century claimed at least one trembling victim from Landican'.

BARNSTON AND THINGWALL

An old village in a lush green vale

Most folk I talk to about Barnston remember the place for one thing only - summer Sunday School picnics in the Dale. This lovely place must have resounded to the clamour of children's voices in the olden days, when the steam train brought them from Wirral's towns to Storeton Station in this, the rural heart of the peninsula. And the Dale really is a lovely place. The motorist only gets a fleeting glimpse, of course, as he negotiates the hazardous twists and turns through the vale. He, sadly, doesn't see the lush meadows filled in early summer with golden buttercups; or the bluebells, celandine and wood-anemones flouncing in the breeze beneath the shade of beeches and birches: 'A Surrey in miniature', as one early writer called it.

Apart from the Dale, there is little else of note in Barnston; it has no great claims to fame, and the church and inn are very ordinary. Despite that, it is a very attractive village, its rather special qualities being summed up 50 years ago by a local writer: 'To those who know and love every inch of it, Barnston is set in one of the most beautiful spots in the whole of our beautiful Wirral, a little haven the placid surface of whose existence is at present threatened with disturbance by those who see in its unprogressiveness wide scope for activity'. Let us sincerely hope not.

*   *   *

If Barnston has little, adjoining Thingwall has even less. It is typical Wirral suburbia, albeit quite pleasant. Yet at Cross Hill, a high point off the main road to Chester, was the meeting-place of the Danish or Norse settlers; here, once or twice a year, our forebears met to formulate and review matters of law relating to this part of Cheshire. And that's it. Mortimer summed up the place in 1847: 'There is nothing in Thingwall, which stands high and is almost destitute of trees, deserving the least notice'.

STORETON

Country village with an old hall and ancient trackways

All ways meet at Storeton: roadways, footpaths, bridleways and causeways. One of the most fascinating is that known as the 'Roman road' or 'the monks' stepping stones', which leads across the fields to Prenton. One section is paved with large, time-worn stone slabs, which no doubt gave it its local name. However, as one old writer stated: 'That an occasional monk may have stepped along these stones is quite probable, and there can be little doubt that sometimes a stray Roman may have used this very lane nearly two thousand years ago but it has no more right to either name than any other lane in the neighbourhood'.

Storeton must have been an important place in the past, but there is little here now save a few cottages, farms, and the old hall. This was the home of the original master-forester of Wirral whose official badge and title of office was a brass-tipped hunting horn, now widely used to represent Wirral in a much wider context than a hunting-ground for game.

These fine, green, open lands round and about Storeton seem far removed from the hustle and bustle of life on the other side of the tree-clothed ridge away to the east; but that contrast is, of course, one of the nicest things about Wirral.

The Wirral Horn

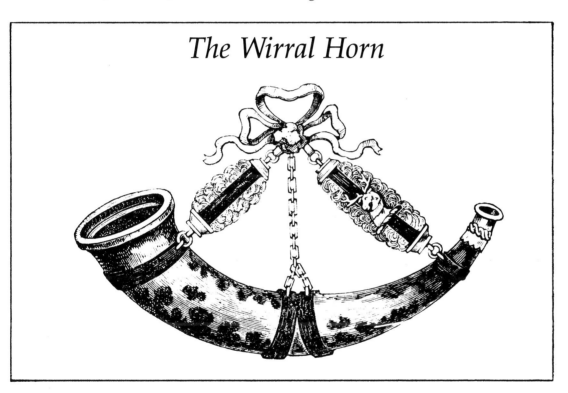

BRIMSTAGE

Rural village with an old hall and its own Cheshire Cat

'To grin like a Cheshire cat' is a saying used far outside its county origins - and, incidentally, long before its appearance in 'Alice in Wonderland'. Just what these origins are is unknown, but could they possibly be here in this tiny Wirral village?

'The long and straggling village stands in a rather peculiar situation, the houses of which it is composed being nearly all placed on one side of a ravine which extends through the hamlet, and down the centre of which a rivulet runs; this, after heavy rains, is the cause of much inconvenience to the inhabitants.' That was written 150 years ago: today the river still runs through the village, but probably the greatest inconvenience is the traffic which speeds through, barely negotiating the tortuous bends. In the past, most traffic passed through Brimstage, but now much of it stops here, and this is where our 'Cheshire Cat' story continues.

The visitors come to Brimstage Hall, which in recent years has become the centre of a thriving crafts centre. Farm buildings have been converted to workshops and sales-rooms, all with a rustic touch, and dominating it all is ancient Brimstage Hall. To even the casual eye the place looks old, and it comes as no surprise to learn that parts of the tower may date back to the 14th century or earlier. That it was a part of a defensive building is obvious: it sits on a slight eminence with commanding views across the Wirral countryside towards the hills of Wales. But, as a writer stated 75 years ago, 'It was not built for mere enjoyment of the view, we may be sure, and even now a few faggots lighted on its crown could lift a flame high enough to be seen from far-away Moel Fammau, rising clear above the hills'.

And the Cheshire Cat? Well, in a room below the tower sits a grotesque corbel of a grinning face. This has been connected with the ancestry of the hall - the Domvilles - whose coat-of-arms included a red lion. Could it be that the mason who carved the arms depicted the lion more as a cat, with a particularly strange grin? Perhaps 'Lewis Carroll' - a Cheshire man - knew of the Brimstage stone and included it in his story. By the way, the village boasted an inn bearing the name of the 'Red Cat' until this century.

This part of Wirral is good farming country, with well-managed fields as far as the eye can see. Gone though are the old, small, irregular fields of the past with their small patches of flower-filled turf and tangled hedgerows. In their place has arisen a patch-work of large, prairie-like fields, almost clinical in their sterile culture of limited crop-types and low, neatly-trimmed hedges and fences. A far cry from the 'bleak and moorish' appearance of two centuries ago. The field-paths remain, though, and these provide a splendid network of walks to other villages in this rural heart of Wirral.

Brimstage Hall

THORNTON HOUGH

Church, cottages and smithy set around a village green

Set amidst lush pastures and fine woodland in the rural heart of Wirral, Thornton Hough is regarded by many folk as the gem of Wirral villages. On a warm summer's evening the village, with its parish church, blacksmith's forge, and half-timbered cottages dotted picturesquely around the village green, wears an air of pastoral peace and tranquility. Surely this place is centuries old; this must be a fine example of an old Cheshire village?

Yet the truth is that Thornton Hough as we see it today is, almost entirely, less than a hundred years old! Note this description of the place as seen by a traveller in 1847: 'the village presents a very unpleasant appearance, and though it possesses a few tolerably good houses, the greater portion are of a very inferior description.'

Into this poor Cheshire village came, first, Joseph Hirst, a retired Yorkshire woollen merchant. Between 1866 and 1877 he built the parish church, the vicarage, church school, and the group of cottages and shops behind the church. These and other changes caused a later traveller to remark, 'Thornton Hough presents a collection of mansions and villas second to none in the Hundred.' Yet the biggest change was still to come, and all to do with soap!

In 1889 the first Viscount Leverhulme had started work on the village and works of Port Sunlight; a few years later he bought Thornton Manor, a large mansion on the outskirts of Thornton Hough. Within a few years of moving into the Manor he had knocked down the old village buildings and in their places he built houses like those at Port Sunlight. He also built a school, a girls' orphanage, shops, a club, and a village smithy, complete with spreading chestnut tree! The Congregational church, in imitation Norman style, was commissioned by Lever, who insisted that no expense be spared in its design and erection.

Take a leisurely stroll around this lovely village; admire the buildings, gardens, and green (the place has won the 'Best Kept Village' award on several occasions). And, while you wander, bear in mind the following thought: 'The village is almost unique in that during the lifetime of many of the older residents, the village scene has changed completely; gone are the village pump, the workshop of the village cobbler who made hand-sewn boots; the toll-bar, the woodman's hut with its axe displayed on the side. In their place has arisen one of the most charming villages of the English country scene.'

Opposite top:
the Seven Stars Inn
and Parish Church,
Thornton Hough.
Note the two clock-
faces on the church
tower; the original
one could not be seen
from the east, so
another had to be
installed above it

Opposite below:
Thornton Manor
gatehouse

Springtime in Thornton Hough: in the foreground, the village green. On the skyline Lever's 'Norman' style church and Hurst's parish church

Summer evening outside the Wheatsheaf Inn, Raby village

RABY

An old inn amongst the farming community of Wirral's smallest village

Visitors and newcomers to Wirral go to Raby expecting to find the waters of Raby Mere lapping at the edge of the village. Don't make the same mistake - the lake is some two miles distant from the village of Raby. Village? Can you call a collection of farms and cottages, and an old inn, a village? Raby is a hamlet, a mere blink of the eyes on the twisty road across the 'saddle of Wirral' between Bromborough and Neston. This is real countryside, good Cheshire farming country intersected by narrow lanes and muddy field-paths.

Perhaps this is what attracts folk from the towns and suburbs on fine summer evenings and at weekends to the Wheatsheaf, a country inn in every sense of the word. Sit outside the front of the Wheatsheaf with your pint, and chances are you'll have the company of a Friesian or two not far away, while the hens chuckle about your feet. This was a real wayside inn, a traveller's rest, a farm-hand's pub until it was discovered by townies as a nice place to go for a taste of the rural atmosphere while relaxing over a drink or two. Yet it has not been spoilt. The thatch and whitewash are real enough, and the inside is as rough and gloomy as you might expect in a building dating back to the early years of the seventeenth century.

There's little else to see in Raby. In summer the cottage gardens are bright with old-fashioned flowers, and the scent of may-blossom fills the air. Historically the name Raby seems to represent the boundary of the Scandinavian occupation of Wirral 1,000 years ago. Other places in Wirral may change, but Raby seems to sleep on, regardless. We'll leave the place with the words of a visitor about the turn of the century, which may have been written today: 'Raby Village, its walls grey-green as the trunks of its apple-trees, is quietly prosperous. Its centre is the Wheatsheaf Inn, a thick-walled old house standing away from the road on a stoney causeway. The sight of this old place, with its quaint sign, low-browed ingle, and cavernous stone stairways, is sufficient to stir a very somnolent imagination. It has stood facing the moorland wind for years, and there is no reason why it should not so stand for centuries to come, unless (and such crimes are not unknown) it should be deliberately razed to the ground'.

RABY MERE AND DIBBINSDALE

Scenic beauty of lake, woods and winding country lanes

Springtime in Dibbinsdale: a sunny April morning with a north-westerly breeze sending bundles of fleecy-white clouds racing across a blue sky. Down in the valley the brook sparkles on its way to the Pool. In the reed-beds a lone heron stands stock-still, a grey-white statue awaiting some passing prey. The electric blue of a kingfisher flashes above the river and is gone. In the woods pussy-willows and catkins shake in the quiet breeze, a touch of colour against the dark tones of the larger trees. Fresh, green, new life springs from the decayed woodland floor: wood-anemones, celandines, marsh-marigolds, ferns, bluebell leaves, are all awakening with the new-found warmth in the air. Soon the

woods will darken as the leaves burst into life, and the lovely flowers of the woods will be no more. These precious moments in this green paradise are ours for today - tomorrow will bring its own problems, its own joys. This is a day to enjoy for its own sake, with no thought for tomorrow.

The people of Bromborough are amongst the luckiest in Wirral, for they have on their doorstep this tangled wilderness of wooded river valleys, wet meadows and Wirral's largest sheet of water. These river valleys radiate from Raby Mere like spokes from a wheel - ancient, native woodlands rich in flowers that have taken centuries to root and spread. Can there be a sight more glorious than these bluebell woods in May - a shimmering haze of blue filling the air with that pervasive perfume so characteristic of these wild hyacinths.

But not only the woods, the brooks and the meadows - Raby Mere too. Hard to believe that this is not a natural lake - so well does it blend in with the surrounding woods and pastures. Long, long ago the brook was dammed up for the water mill below, and thus Raby Mere was formed. The works of man are rarely as beautiful as this: 'Nowhere else is there such a varnish on the holly hedges, and bluebells crowd so thickly around your feet that you shrink from treading down the azure belfry. Tea can be obtained at every cottage in the dale; but not on Sunday - neither crumb nor crust nor cup can you get for fear, love or money. Raby Mere still remains the same sylvan glade, so closely interwoven with the golden memories of youth and childhood.'

WILLASTON

Old and new in the heart of the Wirral countryside

It is easy to pass through Willaston without noticing anything of particular interest: it seems a nice enough place, with a good blend of houses and shops - but little else. That's not surprising, for the very situation of Willaston - right in the centre of the peninsula - makes it a village one passes through on the way to somewhere else, and not a place to visit for its own sake. And that is sad. For Willaston really is a most interesting place.

Take its name, for a start. It was one of the first places in Wirral to be colonised by the invading Anglo-Saxons during the 7th century, and such was its importance that it gave its name, as Wilaveston, to the entire Hundred of Wirral. And not far from here, by the Chester High Road, lies the so-called 'Wirral Stone', thought by some to mark the old assembly or meeting-place of the Wirral Hundred; yet others think it may simply be an old mounting-block, or perhaps a mile-stone.

Back in the village, it's well worth while to take the fascinating 'Village Trail' which visits places of interest in and around Willaston. At the heart of the village, the Green gives the place a nice, open feel, despite the presence of parked cars, and many folk think this Green was once much bigger, perhaps to accommodate the Hundred Assembly of olden days.

Grouped around the Green is a hotch-potch of buildings old and new, the half-

Opposite:
the autumn glory of a wooded river-valley between Raby Mere and Willaston

125

timbered Red Lion Inn being of particular interest; whilst across the Green the mellow stones of the old hall contrast with, but seem quite undisturbed by, the new buildings sprouting all around!

One of the best things about Willaston is that it is only a few minutes' walk in any direction to real, mid-Wirral, open countryside - typical Cheshire pasture-land bisected by neatly-kept hedges and grazed by healthy-looking cows. Dominating the scene, away to the north, is the sail-less tower of Willaston Mill, the last of several mills occupying sites hereabouts since the 14th century. Legend has it that one old Willaston miller was so efficient that he had the corn cut and threshed in the early hours of the morning, immediately grinding it and making it into bread, and delivering it to London the same night!

In other directions, you will stumble upon other reminders of the past - Street Hey, thought to be a small part of the old Roman road from Chester to the northern part of the peninsula; and the beautifully preserved old railway station of Hadlow Road, on the Wirral Way.

All village trails return to the village Green, always a scene of activity and a focal point for local folk on fine evenings. This has always been so, of course, and we are reminded of this by the words of a visitor to Willaston about 80 years ago who noticed the old village pumps standing disused by the Green: 'A venerable man sunning him-self in a fragrant garden near the inn remembered them. "It was a merry village then. The

The early morning sun silhouettes Willaston Mill

maids of all the farms around would come every evening and take away what water would last till the following night - aye, carrying it away in wooden cans on their heads again and again. A real meeting-place it was then."'

*The old
Red Lion Inn
Willaston*

*Winter sunrise
pierces the early
morning mists
which are a
common feature of
this flat mid-
Wirral countryside
of pastures,
hedgerows and
copses*

CAPENHURST, LEDSHAM AND SAUGHALL

A horned lady, nuclear energy, and an ancient pinfold

You can pass through Capenhurst village without ever knowing that there is a huge atomic energy establishment in the area. In fact this neat little village, with its cottages, farm buildings and delightful church, seems entirely rural, with no hint of the twentieth-century works covering acres of land away to the north, and almost engulfing the adjoining tiny hamlet of Ledsham.

There is something else rather special about Capenhurst: it possesses one of only two remaining pinfolds in the peninsula; the other is at Spital. You will find the one at Capenhurst on the west side of the village, at the side of the main road. The village pinfold, or pound, is an ancient institution, where domestic animals were kept until redeemed by their owner. The animals may have been impounded for debt, for aggrievance, or as strays.

Mention may be made, while at Capenhurst, of an old family whose longevity seems proof of the salubrity of this part of Wirral. They were the five Maddock brothers, farmers, whose ages ranged from 86 to 94. Their combined ages were 450 years, giving an average age of 90! 'They were all, from the youngest to the eldest, perfectly competent to manage their business. They were good horsemen, active pedestrians, and capable of reading without the aid of glasses.'

From some parts of Capenhurst you can see the sails of the old Saughall windmill, often called the Gibbet Mill from the time when two Irish labourers were hanged from a nearby ash-tree for robbing and murdering a traveller. This windmill is probably one of the 'Two Mills' which give the area its well-known name. And the other? Well, there may have been a windmill at Capenhurst; and there was almost certainly a water-mill near Two Mills crossroads.

The villages of Little and Great Saughall are more Chester than Wirral, but are worth mentioning as the birth-place of the celebrated Horned Lady, Mary Davies. This poor woman was born here about the year 1600 and, at the age of about 30, started to grow a strange excrescence out of her head. By the time she was 60, these had taken on the form of real horns, which fell off and grew again every four years or so. The horns were 'in show and substance much like rams' horns, solid and wrinkled, but sadly grieving the old woman, especially upon the change of weather'. Despite this, Mary Davies lived to a ripe old age, for she was exhibited in London at the age of 81! Her horns were evidently much sought-after, for we know that 'one an English Lord obtained and presented to the French King'. Medical opinion of the day was that the horns were caused by Mrs Davies wearing her hat too tightly on her head. You have been warned!

*Opposite:
country life
epitomised at
Capenhurst, with
church, farms and
cottages on a fine
summer's day*

*Mary Davies,
the horned lady
of Saughall,
from an
old engraving*

Saughall adjoins the township of Shotwick Park, a medieval deer-park whose curved boundaries are still evident and, right at the western edge of which stood the ancient castle of Shotwick. A few majestic earthworks are all that remain of what was once a mighty and important fortress built on this bloody English-Welsh border, probably by the Normans as one of a line of defences against Welsh invasions. In those days, of course, the castle was at the Dee's edge, its waters swirling through the moat as an added defence. The great kings of those times passed this way from time to time: Henry II in 1156, Henry III a hundred years later, and Edward I in 1278. The old site today looks out, not across the swirling Dee waters, but across acres of agricultural sea-land, with the outline of the Welsh hills forming a fitting back-cloth in the far distant west.

*Capenhurst
Parish Church*

WIRRAL COUNTRY PARK

From Dee cliff-tops to the heart of the Wirral countryside

'Course of old railway' said the words on the map: having explored other disused railway lines and found the experience quite enjoyable, we decided to give this one a try. The year was 1969. Country Parks were unheard of - there were parks (with lawns and rose beds); and there was countryside (with fields and barbed wire). You were allowed in one, but not the other.

On the map, this old track looked quite promising: it ran alongside the Dee for much of its course, and passed quite near some of our favourite Wirral villages. If we got fed up, or wet, we could always hop on a bus home. In the event we did get tired; we got wet too: but fed-up? No! Perhaps it was the excitement of exploring the unknown; or the hazards of negotiating old railway ironmongery lying hidden in waist-high under-growth. But that day was something special - the beginning of an attachment with part of our heritage which today, perhaps, we take rather for granted.

131

Opposite:
Wirral Country
Park: springtime on
the Caldy section

The Wirral Country Park has the distinction of being one of the first in the land to be recognised as a Country Park following the Countryside Act of 1968. The first local body to see the potential of the old railway line as a recreational area was the Wirral Green Belt Council, and in 1969 Cheshire County Council, with the backing of the Countryside Commission, started work on the old route. The Park was officially opened in October 1973 by Lord Leverhulme, Lord Lieutenant of Cheshire.

In 20 years the Wirral Country Park has grown from that tangled trail threading unnoticed through the Wirral countryside, into the beautiful, fascinating place we know and love today. We all have our own favourite places along the Wirral Way, and our own fond experiences. Here are some of mine.

Cubbins Green on a fresh spring morning. A mild, south-westerly breeze sweeps across the estuary from distant Welsh moors. The gorse buds are showing yellow after the hard frosts of winter, and the willows are draped in golden catkins. Behind, the slopes of Caldy Hill are showing patches of light green; whilst, below our feet, the incoming tide laps gently against the sea defences at the base of the cliffs. Out in the estuary, Hilbre looks a little dismal, shrouded in a light grey mist. A few lone oyster-catchers shriek above our heads, looking for new feeding grounds. Spring is coming to Wirral.

Hadlow Road Station: a bright summer's day. In contrast to the natural beauty of the surrounding countryside, we are sitting on this old station platform. But beauty takes many different forms, and there is a certain quality in these fine old buildings which saw

Wirral Country Park, by Cubbins Green, Caldy

so much life, so much activity in the days when steam-trains halted at these platforms. But listen . . . 'Stop a moment, and imagine. It is 1952. The train will soon be in. You hear its whistle, faint on the wind. Behind you, businessmen and shoppers on their way to the city move aside for a porter pulling a trolley load of mail and country produce. From inside comes the sound of jingling coins and the thud of the date stamp as the clerk issues tickets. A late-comer rushes on to the platform as the train steams in . . .'

Neston rock cutting: a golden October day of clear blue skies and warm, still, hazy air. Shafts of sunlight filter through the bronzing canopy overhead to the gloomy reaches below, highlighting drifts of blood-red berries which have yet escaped the notice of hungry birds. Strange toadstools decorate the yellow, leaf-strewn floor, where a grey squirrel forages for food. Water oozes and drips down the moss-covered walls of this tunnel-like place, to collect in muddy puddles along the pathway. Things rustle in the decaying vegetation all around, and the seasonal smell, that undefinable aroma that belongs only to autumn, pervades the air. A feeling of mystery fills this cathedral-like place, with its stained-glass leaves of bramble, and its gothic arches of sycamore branches.

And, in all of these images of this wonderful place, there is always, in the far-off distance of place and time, an ever-so-faint sound . . . the whistle and hiss of a steam-train, perhaps?

WIRRAL'S WILDLIFE

The beauty of the natural world of the Wirral peninsula

WIRRAL'S WILDLIFE

The beauty of the natural world of the Wirral peninsula

The words and photographs in this book have offered small glimpses into the tremendous wealth of wildlife which exists in Wirral. That so much does exist is quite amazing for such a small place so near to a large population of people. Perhaps it is the variety of natural and man-made habitats which contributes to making the peninsula a home for so many plants, birds and animals.

We have dense woodlands, small streams and miles of hedgerows; some fifty miles of coastline with crumbly cliffs, sandy beaches and grassy dunes; two estuaries of international importance for bird life, with mud-flats and salt-marsh; an offshore island with its associated cliffs, rocky bays and inter-tidal shores; and, of course, we have wind-swept heaths, pools, ponds and pits, and a few grassy meadows.

There is something for the nature-lover all the year round: springtime sees the blooming of our woodland flowers and the influx of migrant birds heading northwards; summer clothes the heaths and meadows with the rich colours of wild-flowers, and the adornment of moths and butterflies; autumn sees the golden colouring of woodland trees, and the massing of wader flocks over the estuaries; whilst even in winter, there are wildfowl in large numbers to be seen on the Dee marshes.

Space does not allow a comprehensive catalogue of all the wildlife to be seen across our peninsula; however, let me give you a few glimpses into some of the places I know and love, and the natural beauty to be found therein.

I start with the wild-flowers of Wirral. In springtime, the ancient woodlands around Dibbinsdale are glorious with patches of wood-anemone, wood-sorrel and the tiny moschatel (also known locally as 'the town hall clock' or 'five-faced bishop' on account of its face-like flowers pointing in all directions). Lesser celandine, too, carpets the lane-sides and hedge-banks all over the peninsula, but particularly around Gayton and Burton. Primroses are scarce now in Wirral, but a few shy clumps survive by the Arrowe Brook, and become more plentiful in the secluded woods and dales around Shotwick.

A little later, bluebells carpet not only the floors of our main woodlands, but also appear in surprising, unsuspected places - on the slopes of Caldy Hill, in Barnston Dale, on the sea-facing grassy slopes about New Brighton, and on the wind-swept turf of Hilbre. About this time of the year, too, the golden flowers of the marsh-marigold adorn our shallower ponds and wet, marshy areas, particularly around Arrowe Park and Brotherton Park. And on the calcareous soils bordering the north Wirral coast, the cowslips survive, despite the encroachment of roads and houses right into their territory.

Opposite: harbinger of spring - snowdrops in Dibbinsdale

As summer draws on, these same cowslip-meadows burst into colour, as ragged-robin, ox-eye daisies, yellow rattle, meadowsweet, speedwells and other meadow-plants come into full bloom. In the damp ditches around here, you will find the rather unique and aptly-named 'yellow button', brought to these parts from South Africa last century by Lady Cust, of nearby Leasowe Castle: 'She had a strong liking for collecting strange plants during her travels and bringing them home for cultivation in her garden. She may have picked up the *Cotula* [yellow button] during her travels, either designedly, or, what is more probable, undesignedly.' Since when this strange little plant has spread all along the north Wirral coast, and has also sprung up in other places too.

A little further away, on the sandy dunes which stretch along the coast from New Brighton right round to Red Rocks, plants of a different kind spring into life: sea-holly, burnet rose, chicory, star-of-Bethlehem; and, if you know where to look, beautiful, majestic orchids of pink and purple.

Late summer sees our heathlands at their best: the slopes of Bidston hill, Caldy hill, Grange hill, Thurstaston hill and Heswall dales are clothed in regal purple; whilst in a

Red Rocks Marsh,
Hoylake.
Flag iris decorate
the shallow pools,
also home of the rare
Natterjack toad

Wet hollow on Thurstaston Hill, a good place for many kinds of wildlife

few damp hollows we may find the insect-eating sundew, the yellow spikes of bog asphodel, the fluffy heads of cotton-grass, or the rare and beautiful marsh gentian.

You know, there is an old Cheshire saying which goes: 'When the gorse is in flower, kissing is in fashion'. Well, we must be a very romantic lot here in Wirral, for, in most years, when the winter is mild, the gorse continues to flower right through the year! What a lovely sight it is, to see these golden-yellow bushes in full bloom around Christmas time and into the New Year.

Where there are flowers and plants, then you will also find moths and butterflies. The cool, northerly location of our peninsula may not give us the variety of butterflies seen in the warmer, southern counties of England; but we can still boast a good share of the common species. In good summers, the flower-filled grasslands above New Brighton's Red Noses and the grassy dunes of Red Rocks are alive with tortoiseshells, common blues, meadow and wall browns, and the gaudy burnet moths. Even in the shady woods around Bromborough, the speckled wood butterfly and the comma butterfly can be seen flitting about in the sunlit glades.

The sight of fungi - mushrooms and toadstools - seems to arouse strong passions of destruction in some folk, for our autumn walks are often littered with the remains of broken plants. It is sad, for we have a rich and colourful variety about us in our woods and meadows. The birch-woods of Caldy, Irby and Thurstaston hills are particularly good places in which to find the beautifully-coloured fly agaric, the tough birch bracket, and many other of our strange fungi.

A book could be written about the bird life of the Wirral peninsula; in fact fifty years ago a book *was* written about the bird life of the Dee estuary alone, by one of the greatest local naturalists of all time, Guy Farrar. He summed up the joys of bird-watching in this part of Wirral: 'How can I envisage in words that insistent call that comes to some of us: the call of the running tide, the longing to set foot once again on the saltings, to smell the tang of the sea air, to hear the sound of rubber boots squelching over soft mud, or the sleepy murmur of ocean rollers breaking on a distant sandbank. In summer heat or winter cold, the estuary draws us to its shingle beaches, its saltings, or its freezing mudflats, to watch the bird life of the foreshore, or to greet the hosts of visitors from the north who make their home on our far-flung coastline during the dead months of the year.'

And the bird-visitors come in their thousands - tens of thousands - to the estuaries flanking our peninsula. Waders - knot, dunlin, redshank, oyster-catcher - feed on the wet mudflats, and roost on the sandbanks and rocks around the coast. The autumn spectacle of wader-flocks over the Dee has been witnessed by famous names in the naturalists' world: Eric Hosking, Eric Simms, Lord Alanbrooke, Roger Peterson; and, of course, even H.R.H. Prince Philip paid occasional secret visits to Hilbre to view the birds.

But the estuaries do not have a monopoly on bird life in Wirral: its woods, heaths and meadows each have their own wealth of birds to enrich the enjoyment of our countryside areas. Gone, alas, are the days when the nightingale sang in Birkenhead Park; that was way back in 1863, but one was also heard in Bromborough and again in Ledsham on several occasions during the latter years of the 19th century.

Of the mammals, surely the invasion of the fox into all areas of Wirral has been the most talked-about in recent years. Once a rarely-seen animal of the remoter country areas, foxes can now be seen, even in the middle of the day, in most parts of the peninsula, and their raucous calls pierce the quietness of the night-time hours in suburban streets. Another invader, the grey squirrel, has all but driven out our native red squirrel: the last one I saw was in Royden Park about 1985, about the same time that I saw one in Burton Woods.

We are fortunate to have badgers resident in Wirral again, for they were evidently extinct here for much of the early part of this century. Coward stated in 1910 that 'In Wirral, if the badger now exists at all, it is rare'; and a magazine article of 1934 stated that 'Readers will remember that in one of the earlier issues I hinted that badgers were again in Wirral, and I have now definite proof that they are back again in two different localities. This is a most interesting discovery. Badgers have always been sufficiently rare in these parts as to cause comment in certain circles, and as the last reported occurrence was in 1893, I do not propose to name the present localities'. The efforts of badger preservation groups to protect these lovely animals are most worthy of promotion.

When the late Norman Ellison, naturalist and local historian, wrote in 1955 about the

Opposite: waders on the Dee estuary, one of the most important estuaries in Europe for bird-life

140

presence of otters in Wirral, he mentioned that they still survived in the marshy lands around the River Gowy, along the southernmost edge of the peninsula. He also mentioned occasional otters being found in the 1950s in Moreton, on the marsh by Burton Point, and even swimming in the waters of the Dee estuary!

Bats have become the subject of much interest locally, with regular 'bat watches' being attended by dozens of dedicated enthusiasts. At Dibbinsdale, one branch of the 'otter's bridge' in Brotherton Park has been converted for use as a bat roost.

Back on the Dee estuary, the colony of grey seals is an exciting aspect of wildlife and one of fairly recent origins: before the 1930s there had only been an occasional sighting, but between then and the 1960s the colony grew steadily to reach its maximum number of about 200, since when it has declined to about half that number. To watch these fascinating creatures, either sunning themselves in a group on the West Hoyle Bank, or swimming about the deep waters off Hilbre, is one of the most enjoyable experiences I know.

Mention has already been made of the plants of Red Rocks Marsh Nature Reserve; but did you know that, in the brackish pools and reed-beds, there exists a rare amphibian, the *bufo calamita*? Better known as the natterjack toad, this elusive little creature is renowned for its loud and repetitive croaking during the mating season, the sound of which, if not previously experienced, is quite unbelievable in its intensity. The decline of the natterjack in recent decades is sad: Coward stated in 1910 that 'In the 1880s and 90s the natterjack was abundant on the Wallasey sandhills, and on the low-lying land behind the Leasowe embankment.' The colony at Red Rocks is its last haunt on the Wirral peninsula.

My writings and researches into the many aspects of local life, past and present, take me into many corners of Wirral. However, my favourite times are those idle hours spent amongst the natural things around us: on the soft turf of Hilbre, accompanied only by the plants and birds; in the quiet, green woods of Dibbinsdale; walking the grassy, flower-bedecked heights above New Brighton's Red Noses; or perhaps ambling along the leafy, flowery old tracks and footpaths which criss-cross the peninsula. The wildlife of Wirral is beautiful, and precious. I hope it will be for ever so.

POSTSCRIPT

*Some final thoughts about the future of
the Wirral peninsula*

POSTSCRIPT

Some final thoughts about the future of the Wirral peninsula

The images of Wirral portrayed in this book are a personal expression of just a small but unique corner of England. They also happen to be the pleasant images.

There are also other aspects of Wirral life not depicted here. We have our high-rise flats, derelict factories, and rubbish-strewn sites as in any other well-populated area of the world. They must not be forgotten amidst the wealth of beauty which comprises so much of our peninsula. These less-pleasant images must be dealt with, so that we may not approach any corner of Wirral with averted eyes, pretending that it does not exist.

Other, less obvious aspects of life in the peninsula deserve attention too: the continuing demand for green-field sites for housing, factories and retail stores; pollution of land and water; and the constant pressures on the Dee and Mersey estuaries for recreation and leisure, for commerce and of course for barrage and crossing schemes. Both estuaries may be barraged within a generation, with the associated threats to landscape and habitats.

Attention should be paid, too, to our towns and villages. Each has its own identity, a rich diversity of architectural styles and building materials, yet still very English, very Wirral-like. We must avoid those gradual and subtle changes which are tending to rob our villages of their unique character; their Englishness must be retained. Traditions also form an important part of our heritage: we must fight to maintain those aspects of traditional life which are historically sound and add to the quality of life. I include here the need to maintain traditional county boundaries (Wirral is in Cheshire!), and even the unique identity of Wirral as the Wirral Peninsula, and not just 'The Wirral'.

Patterns of country life are changing too, with ponds and hedgerows disappearing, and farm buildings undergoing conversion to housing accommodation. Wirral will soon have few working farms unless this trend is reversed.

On the positive side, it is heartening to see the increasingly active roles played by local amenity and conservation groups, whose protesting but constructive voices are being heard with greater attention than ever in the past. It is good, too to see an increasing awareness of the richness of our heritage in all its forms, by ordinary folk, both young and old. Such recognition can only augur well for the future of a small peninsula such as this.

And so let this positive note be our last image of Wirral - of a place beautiful to look at, pleasant to live in, and with a unique heritage worthy to be handed down to the generations to follow.

APPENDIX 1

WIRRAL'S PLACE-NAMES

Images of Wirral has taken you around the peninsula's towns and villages; but the very names of these places, and their origins, makes a fascinating study in itself. Here is a list of place-names in Wirral, with their probable meanings:

Arrowe: at the shieling

Barnston: Beornwulf's farm

Bebington: farm called after Bebba

Bidston: rock with a dwelling

Birkenhead: headland with birch trees

Brimstage: Bruna's river-bank

Bromborough: Bruna's stronghold

Burton: farm or enclosure at a fortification

Caldy: cold arse, or cold islands

Capenhurst: wooded hill at a look-out place

Childer Thornton: thorn-tree farm of the young men or children

Claughton: farm on a hillock

Eastham: village in the east

Ellesmere Port: the port on the Ellesmere Canal

Ford: the river-crossing

Frankby: Frenchman's farm

Gayton: goat farm

Greasby: stronghold at a wood

Heswall: hazel spring

Hilbre: Hildeburg's island

Hooton: farm at a hill or promontory

Hoylake: the lake at the hill of sand

Irby: farm of the Irishmen

Landican: Tegan's church

Ledsham: Leofede's homestead

Liscard: hall at the rock

Meols: the sandhills

Moreton: farm at a marsh

Ness: at the promontory

Neston: farm or enclosure at the headland

Noctorum: dry hill

Overchurch: church by the shore

Overpool: pool by the shore

Oxton: farm or enclosure where oxen are kept

Pensby: farm at a hill called Penn (top)

Poulton: farm by a pool or creek

Prenton: Pren's farm

Puddington: farm called after Puta

Raby: village at a boundary

Saughall: corner where willows grow

Seacombe: valley by the sea

Shotwick: hamlet at a steep promontory

Spital: the hospital

Stanlow: stone hill or rock hill

Stanney: rock island

Storeton: the great farmstead

Sutton: south farm

Thingwall: field where an assembly meets

Thornton Hough: thorn-tree farm/ family of de Hogh

Thurstaston: Thorsteinn's farmstead

Tranmere: cranes' sandbank

Upton: farm on a hill

Wallasey: island of the Welshmen or Britons

West Kirby: the westerly village with a church

Whitby: the white manor

Willaston: Wiglaf's farm

Woodbank: the wooded hillside

Woodchurch: church in a wood or wooden church

The study of place-name derivations is fraught with problems, and not all scholars will agree with these meanings; however, we shall probably never know the truth behind the origins of most of these names.

But what about the origin of **'Wirral'**, the name by which our peninsula is known? This seems to be 'the nook or corner where the bog myrtle grows'. There is no bog myrtle growing in Wirral today, but analysis of pollen grains from the ancient peat-beds at Meols shows that it did grow here in times past.

APPENDIX 2

A POTTED HISTORY OF WIRRAL

The situation of the Wirral peninsula, enjoying the benefits of a mild climate, easy access to the sea, and seclusion from the more traumatic events of history, has attracted men to make their home here down the ages. We know that Stone Age man lived here, from finds on Thurstaston Hill and elsewhere. During the Bronze Age, and until the time of the Romans, Wirral was occupied by a powerful Celtic tribe known as the Cornovii.

The Romans occupied Chester about AD 70, and traces of their occupation in Wirral have been found from time to time. In 1834 workmen quarrying on the hill known as the Arno, in Oxton, found a number of small coins bearing the heads of Antoninus and Victorinus. Storeton Quarry may have been used by the Romans, for its stone was used to sculpture monuments, the remains of which have been found and can be seen in Chester Museum. Coins have been found at many other parts of the peninsula during recent years.

The greatest evidence of the Roman occupation in Wirral is, however, the large number of articles found along the shore at Meols, indicating an extensive Roman settlement. It appears that this settlement was connected by road with Chester, some twenty miles away; the route is uncertain, but it probably left Chester by the line of the present Parkgate road as far as Mollington, and then continued past Capenhurst to Ledsham. Its course from Ledsham is less certain, but a road-like surface has been excavated at Street Hey, near Willaston, and there is a lane near Raby which is on the line to Meols. Part of an ancient road, possibly Roman, has also been discovered in Greasby. There may have been another Roman road running from Monks' Ferry, on the Mersey shore, by way of Bridge Street towards Bidston and the coast at Meols. In 1850 a bridge was discovered by workmen converting Wallasey Pool into docks; this appeared to be Roman in origin, and may have been part of this route. The bridge was of solid oak beams supported by stone piers, its ends resting on solid rock at the sides of the creek. The length of the bridge was about one hundred feet. From the depth of the silt burying the bridge (about thirty feet), it must have been buried for centuries.

In the spring of 1991 a probable Roman homestead was partially excavated in Irby, the first of its kind to be found in Wirral.

The Romans left about AD 410, and Wirral was occupied by the Britons, who lived undisturbed for about two hundred years. The Anglo-Saxons under Ethelfrith, the Anglian king of Northumbria, laid waste Chester in AD 613 and soon took over most of Wirral, with the exception of Wallasey. Many Wirral villages owe their names to these people, especially those ending in "ham" or "ton", both meaning a home or homestead.

All was peaceful in Wirral for over two hundred years, but in the latter years of the ninth century the Norsemen, the Vikings of the North, invaded our shores. We gain an insight into the character of these wild people, from the Anglo-Saxon Chronicle:

> They reached a waste city in Wirral, which is called Legceaster [Chester]. They besieged the fort from outside for some two days and took all cattle that were without there, and slew the men they were able to intercept without the fort and burnt all the corn, and with their horses devoured the pasture in the whole neighbourhood.

The Norsemen were apparently attracted to Wirral because of its excellent harbours and proximity to the sea, for there is little evidence of their having occupied the rest of Cheshire. They settled along the Dee side of the peninsula, and along the sea coast, giving their villages names such as West Kirby, Frankby and Irby. They also introduced their own system of local government, and probably met at Thingwall, an area of high ground in the northern part of the peninsula. At their annual "Thing", or parliament, new laws were made, and other business of the area was transacted. In spite of their ways, it seems that the Norsemen soon settled down and became one people with their English cousins.

The Doomsday survey of 1085-6 shows that Wirral at that time was more densely populated than most other parts of England. There was very little woodland: one at Mollington, a large area at Tranmere, and a small one at Prenton. This shortage of timber was soon rectified, for Wirral was afforested from Norman times until the middle of the fourteenth century. At least, plenty of tree cover was provided for the preservation of game; it is most unlikely that the whole of the peninsula was covered with trees.

Wirral's proximity to Chester had a profound effect on the history of the Dee side of the peninsula during the fourteenth, fifteenth and sixteenth centuries. Hundreds of years before Liverpool's rise to fame as a great port, Chester was providing facilities for trade with Ireland, Spain, and Germany. Seagoing vessels would "lay-to" at the mouth of the Dee, awaiting favourable winds and tides. But the Dee started to silt up from Chester northwards towards the estuary. Harbouring facilities moved to Burton, Neston, Parkgate, Gayton, Dawpool, West Kirby and Hoylake. The Dee side overshadowed the Mersey side of the peninsula for over three hundred years. Adventurous plans were proposed to overcome the silting-up of the estuary . One was put forward in 1857 by Sir John Rennie, who planned to cut a ship canal, 20 feet deep, from a point between Thurstaston and Heswall, to run along the length of Wirral to Chester. This and other schemes came to nothing. Deeside was dying; and Liverpool was growing as a port of international importance, offering good communications by road and canal to the rest of the country, and a safer, more sheltered harbour for shipping.

The growth of Liverpool signalled the start of a new era for Wirral; an era of tremendous growth and rapid change. For as Liverpool grew as a centre of trade and commerce, its merchants and businessmen looked across the Mersey to the sandy shores and green fields of Wirral, and many "crossed over" to make their homes in Birkenhead. Ferries, trains, docks and commerce soon followed. Between 1810 and 1841 the population of Birkenhead leapt from 109 to a staggering 8,000. As the Mersey side of the peninsula became more industrialised, many moved out of the dirt and grime to the greener parts of Wirral. Growth was naturally greatest along the rail routes - the opening of the Hoylake line in 1866 enabled city-weary Liverpool businessmen to live within sight, sound and smell of the sea. This growth has continued to the present day: rural, land-based communities are disappearing under the spreading tide of suburbia. Nine hundred years ago there were about 2,000 people in the whole of Wirral; its population is now approaching half a million.

APPENDIX 3

A TOUR OF WIRRAL IN 1600

Images of Wirral has taken you on a tour of the Wirral peninsula, in words and photographs. Nearly 400 years ago, another 'tour of Wirral' was written, by a man called William Webb. Despite the archaic language, it makes fascinating reading, and it is interesting to note his comments about the places we know so well today:

'I have laboured to cast the Hundred of Wirral by the dimensions thereof into some resemblance, and though, geometrically considered, it comes nearest to the figure of a long square, or rather a rhomboid, yet because the long sides are not straight lines, nor the opposite ends equal in their distance, we must take it, as it is, irregular; and the nearest resemblance that I can give it, is the sole of a lady's left-foot pantafle, for the furthest north-west end, compassed with the sea, falls somewhat round; then it narrows itself both ways, and between *Bebbington* on the east, and *Oldfield* on the west side, falls narrow of the sole; then it widens itself either way to *Stanney*, on the one side, and Burton on the other, where it is broadest; then narrowing again till it points with the tip of the toe upon Chester liberties. The Welch Britons call it Killgurry, because it is an angle. That it was in old time a forest, I think cannot be doubted, but that it should not be inhabited, or disforested, till Edward the Third's time, that I suppose to be true but in part; for the very antiquity of the church, some castles, monasteries, and the very manurage (manorage) of the most part of it yet appearing argue, the contrary.

But I will not contend, for it sufficeth me that I can boast in behalf of the inhabitants there now, and of their industrious predecessors too, that it is at present one of the most fertile parts, and comparable, if not exceeding, any other so much in quantity of the whole county besides. And this will our weekly market of Chester for corn and fish make good for me, and if I add flesh too, I should not miss it much.

To proceed with the description of it, I shall need to lead you but one walk over the length of it, and back again, which I will covenant to dispatch with much brevity, if I may in my walk make some indentures on either hand, as these jovial fellows we see sometimes do, when, coming out of the Tavern, they indent their journies down the street, to survey their friends on either side.

We will here set in, at the tip of the toe, which comes to the Stone-bridge almost at Chester; and first, we will follow that water dividing this from Bolton hundred, which will bring us a little behind *Upton* to *Chorlton*, and then to the *Lea*, a fair house and fine demesne, so called, and hath been the mansion for some descents of the Glaziers, esquires, of special note and good account. And next unto it lies *Backford* town and church, and hard by it the seat of our worthy prothonotary Henry Berkenhead, esquire, a gentleman whom the whole Country most deservedly acknowledges to have inherited, together with his place, that humanity and fair deportment that were in his fathers and ancestors before him. From whence, as we go, we see on the west of us *Capenhurst*, a fine lordship, belonging to the houses of Cholmondeley and of Poole, and in the same one gentleman's seat.

By our brook lies *Croughton*, a member of the lordship of John Hurleston, esquire; and from thence we come to *Stoke*, a little parish church adjoining to that fair desmesne and ancient seat of the Bunburies, of good worship, called *Staney-hall*, and which may be glad of the worthy present owner, Sir Henry Bunbury, knight, whose grave and well-disposed courses procure unto him a special good estimation for his endeavours to do good in public government, and his more private affairs also.

We turn us now towards our journey more westward, passing by *Whitby*; and from whence it may seem the Whitbys derived their name; of whom this gentleman that now bears part in the government of this city has advanced their names to no mean degree of deserved estimation.

Then holding our course we go by *Great Sutton*, a goodly lordship, and where hath been a famous seat called Sutton Court, the inheritance now of Sir Robert Cholmondely; and upon our other hand *Pool*, a fair ancient seat, with a park, of which the long-coutinued race of the Pools have borne that name, and it is very probable have been the ancestors of some very great families of that name in other counties; the present owner there John Pool, esquire. Near unto which we see also *Stanlow*, now a farm of the said Mr. Pool's.

But there was a Monastery founded by the famous Lacy, constable of Chester, about the year 1173, taking the name from *Staney-hill*, but for the unruliness of the Mersey-Water they misliked their seat there, and found means to be translated from thence to Whaley, in Lancashire.

We come next to *Hooton*, a goodly ancient manor and fair part, which, ever since the reign of King Richard the Second, hath been the seat of the Stanleys of Hooton, gentlemen of great dignity and worth, deriving their pedigree from Allan Silvester, upon whom Ranulph the first, Earl of Chester bestowed the bailiwick of the *Forest of Wirral*, and delivered unto him a horn, to be a token of his gift; from whence we gather that Wirral was holden to be a place of no mean aceount in those times; where have continued the same Stanleys in a direct succession, and was lately possessed by a very worthy and noble-minded knight, Sir Rowland Stanley, who lived there to the age, I have heard, of near one hundred years, and lived to be the oldest knight in this land; which I note the rather to approve the healthfulness of the place, and where his fourth generation, his son's son's son was at the time of his decease. Near unto which stands *Eastham*, the parish church and lordship.

Next beyond it we leave on our left hand *Brinstone*, (*Brimstage*) and so come to *Pooton*, or *Poulton*, of which name there is another township, from which this is distinguished by the name of Lancelot, and the next to that is *Brumbrough*, a pretty town, with a chapel; and therein Daniel Bavand, esquire, hath a fair house and demesne; next which lies *Nether Bebbington* and *Over Bebbington*, the precincts whereof take up in this tract a large extent; the one a church town with a fair church and goodly parsonage, the other a member of the parish where John Minshal, esquire, of Minshall, hath great store of fair possessions.

Upon our left hand we leave *Stoorton*, a lordship, and so go by *Prenton*, where one race of the Hawkenhals have a fine house and demesne; the present owner thereof John Okenhall, esquire. Beyond which lieth *Lanian*, or *Liandecan*, a township with pretty farms in it, the lands of Sir Richard Wilbraham, knight and baronet; and from thence we go next to *Woodchurch*, a parish church and a neat parsonage by it; beneath which, looking towards the *Mersey* again, lies a goodly vale and pleasant track in which we may see *Upton*, a fine lordship, wherein stand the house and demesne, where a long descent of gentlemen have had continuance, sprung from the house of Bould, of Bould in Lancashire, the now owner thereof Peter Bould, esquire, to whom I owe particular respects of love; and next unto this *Oxton*; and then nearer to the Mersey side the township of *Tranmore*; and near to that is a fine seat of that worthy gentleman, whom elsewhere we remembered, John Minshal, of Minshal, esquire, called Derby House.

Thence, on our left hand, we see *Caughton (Claughton)* where Mr. Thomas Powell hath fair lands; and then leaving the ferry, where the passage lies over into Lancashire, to Liverpool, we step over into *Berket-wood*, and where hath been a famous priory, the foundation whereof I am not yet instructed for, but now a very goodly demesne, and which is become (by descent from the Worsleys, men of great possessions) now to a gentleman of much worth, Thomas Powell, esquire, the heir of that ancient seat of Horsley, in the county of Flint.

Beyond which, we have only that other *Poulton* called by the name of *Seacombe*, till we come to the north-western shore, laying upon the Vergivian or Irish Sea, where are situate the township, parish and church of *Kirby, in Walley, or Walsey*, a town which hath fair lands, and where lie those fair sands, or plains, upon the shore of the sea, which, for the fitness for such a purpose, allure the gentlemen and and others oft to appoint great matches and venture no small sums in trying the swiftness of their horses.

And so we come to *Bidston*, a goodly house, demesne, and park of the right honourable William Earl of Derby; which, though it be less than many other seats which his honour hath, wherein to make his residences when he is so pleased; yet for the pleasant situation of this, and the variety of noble delights appendent to it, his lordship seems much to affect the same, and enlargeth the conveniences therein for his pleasure and abode many ways.

Following the circuit of the shire, we come next to *Great Meoles*, which gives name and seat to an ancient family of Meolses; whence we go by *Moreton*, and then by *Saughall Massie*, a very gallant lordship; and leaving *Overchurch* on our left hand, in which we pass by *Newton*, and somewhat beyond that by *Greasby*, where we hold on nearer the shore, and take with us *West Kirby*: here in the utmost western nook of this promontory, divided from the land, lies that little barren island called *Ilbree*, or *Hilbree*; in which it is said there was sometime a cell of monks, though I scarce believe it; for that kind of people loved warmer seats than this could ever be.

From thence we come next to the *Grange*, which I would rather think to be that seat where those monks eat their beef and brewis, and which is now possessed by William Glegg, esquire, being descended to him from his ancestors; upon the side of this to the east lies *Frankley (Frankby)*, a large township, and so we come to the two townships *Great and Little Caldy*.

Near unto which lies the station or landing place for their boats and barges, with their laden aud unladen commodities, called the *Red-bank*; so I take it from the colour of the rock upon the shorebrink; and near unto this lies *Irby*, another fair lordship, wherein the Balls, freeholders, have a good seat. And we come thence to *Thurstanton*, the ancient seat of the Whitmores of *Thurstanton*, the owner now Whitmore, esquire; which race, whether they had their beginning from the city of Chester, in which have been many mayors of that name, or that from them came the name into Chester, their own evidence, wherewithal I am not acquainted, can better declare it than I can. On the east side of it lies *Barnston*, whence it is like the Barnstons, gentlemen in Broxton hundred, had their own name first; and upon the shore side we come next to the *Oldfield*, where we said the narrowest place of the hundred is supposed; and it is like hath given name to these gentlemen, the Oldfields, of whom mention has been made before.

Our next remove is to *Heswall*, or *Hesselwall*, a town where stand the parish church and parsonage, finely situated; and there extends to it a fair lordship of *Thornton Mayow*, and *Raby*, another very pleasant view of a large precinct.

But near the sea side we come to *Gayton*, the seat of that ancient race of Gleggs of Gayton, now the possession of Edward Glegg, esquire, a gentleman well reputed; and next unto lies *Leighton*, in which is seated in a very ancient house and fine demesne, another branch of the Whitmores, of a very great descent, the owner now William Whitmore, esquire. And next neighbour to this are the well-known town, parish church and port of *Great Neston*; and the usual place where our passengers into Ireland do so often lie waiting the leisure of the winds, which makes many people better acquainted with this place than they desire to be, though here be wanting no convenient entertainment, if no other wants be in the way; and here is the station of the ships called *The New Key*, where they embark and disembark both men, horses, kine and all other commodities, on the back of this Neston; to the east lies a large tract of heath and commons, and therein a fair lordship called *Childer Thornton*.

But keeping still our shore we come to *Nesse*. And next to that more landwards *Woollaston*, a great breadth of grounds. And then have we *Burton*, a pretty town. And a landing place by the side of a great brow of a promontory reaching into the sea, they call it *Burton-head*; and next to this we come to that gallant lofty seat of *Puddington*, overlooking the sea, which so far holds on her large breadth unlimited within the mouth of Dee, wherein have continued the race of the Massies, which has been a great name, divided into many branches from that Hamon Massie one of the Earl's barons, and the owner now Sir William Massie, knight, who adds more lustre to the fame of his predecessors, which seat is also beautified with a fine park; a great spacious common, which they vulgarly call *Motherless Heath*, lies eastward behind this a great way further, at the one side whereof we see *Ledsham*; and so we come to *Shotwich*, a little parish church, and near unto it an ancient house that hath belonged to John Hockenhall of Hockenhall, esquire, and so we come to that gallant park called *Shotwickpark*, where sometimes have been, and yet are remaining, the ruins of a fair castle that stands upon the brink of Dee within the park, in which is also a fine lodge for the habitation of the keepers of the Princess Highness's deer in that park, and is in the holding of Sir Richard Wilbraham, aforementioned; from whence we come presently to *Great Saughall*, a fair lordship, and chiefly belonging to His Highness; and *Little Saughall*, another fine township, the lands of sundry freeholders there inhabiting; and along by the precincts of them both, lies a place called anciently *Kingswood*, where now his Highness's tenants have made enclosures, to the great increase of corn for the benefit of the country. And next to this lies, first a goodly ancient seat, upon the brow of Dee banks, called *Blacon Hall*, the name of the whole lordship, the lands of Sir William Norris, knight of the Bath, whom Lancashire hath the most interest in making his chief residence among them, where he hath great possessions: and then adjoineth *Crabhall*, the demesne of William Gamul, a prime alderman of the city of Chester, who there hath a most delicate fine house, to retire into at his pleasure, and choice appendants both for pleasure and profit. And thus we arrive again at the tip of the toe in our description, being to come home presently to the famous city again.

BIBLIOGRAPHY AND SELECT READING

There have been many books written about Wirral over the years; these take many forms, from small leaflets about specific aspects, to full-scale historical-topographical guides to the whole peninsula. The following are those still readily available:

General
The Illustrated Portrait of Wirral, Kenneth J. Burnley, 1987

Historical
The Search for Old Wirral, David Randall, 1984

Sea Images
Castles in the Sand: The Story of New Brighton, Maurice G. Hope, 1982
Fort Perch Rock, K. McCarron, 1991

Dee Images
Hilbre: The Cheshire Island, J. D. Craggs (ed.), 1982
Let's Walk Around Heswall Nos 1 & 2, The Heswall Society
St Peter's Church and Parish, Heswall, Revd Canon K. Lee, 1979
Memories of Heswall, Heswall WEA, 1989
This is Parkgate, G. Place, 1979
Neston and Parkgate, J. Pearson, 1985
Ness Gardens: Bulley's Beginnings to the Present Day, J. K. Hulme, 1988
Burton in Wirral, P. H. W. Booth (ed.), 1984
A Ramble Round Burton, R. Norman Jones (ed.), 1978
The Church at the Ford, Shotwick, L. Whitfield, 1974

Mersey Images
Mersey Maritime Memories, D. & M. Young, 1990
The Forgotten Shores, Maurice G. Hope, 1990
Almost an Island: The Story of Wallasey, Noel Smith, 1990
Birkenhead of Yesteryear, C. Bidston, 1985
Birkenhead Priory: A Closer Look, Williamson Art Gallery & Museum, 1988
Birkenhead Priory, J. McInniss, 1983
The People's Garden: Birkenhead Park, C. E. Thornton, 1984
Birkenhead Park, J. McInniss, 1984
The Changing Years: The Story of Rock Ferry, Rock Ferry Local History Group, 1991
A Guide to Port Sunlight Village, E. Hubbard & M. Shippobottom, 1988

Memories of Old Eastham, E. Stanley
A Walk Around Old Eastham, Eastham Church, 1988
Ellesmere Port: The Making of an Industrial Borough, P. J. Aspinall & D. M. Hudson, 1982
Looking Back at Ellesmere Port, P. O'Brien, 1986

Village & Country Images
The Story of Greasby, J. Williams, 1978
St John the Divine, Frankby with Greasby, A. Nute, 1987
Willaston's Heritage, E. C. Bryan, 1975
Walking the Wirral Way, J. Williams, 1981
The Hooton to West Kirby Branch Line and the Wirral Way, Merseyside Railway History
    Group, 1982
Pubs and Paths, J. Williams, 1982
Wirral Footpaths & Open Spaces Preservation Society Commemorative Booklet, 1988
The Wirral Society - 60 Years On, The Wirral Society, 1988

Miscellaneous
There are many books of old postcards and photos of Wirral. The main series are: *Pictures from the Past* by D. & M. Young; *Yesterday's Wirral* by I. & M. Boumphrey; and those produced by S. B. Publications.

The Wirral Journal is a quarterly magazine produced and edited by K. J. Burnley covering all aspects of local life. Since its inception in 1982 it has grown into a valuable and unique reference collection of almost 2,000 pages of articles relating to Wirral.

Wirral Borough Council's Department of Leisure Services produce a wide range of leaflets and guides to all aspects of the Country Parks; these are usually available from the information centres.

MAP OF WIRRAL

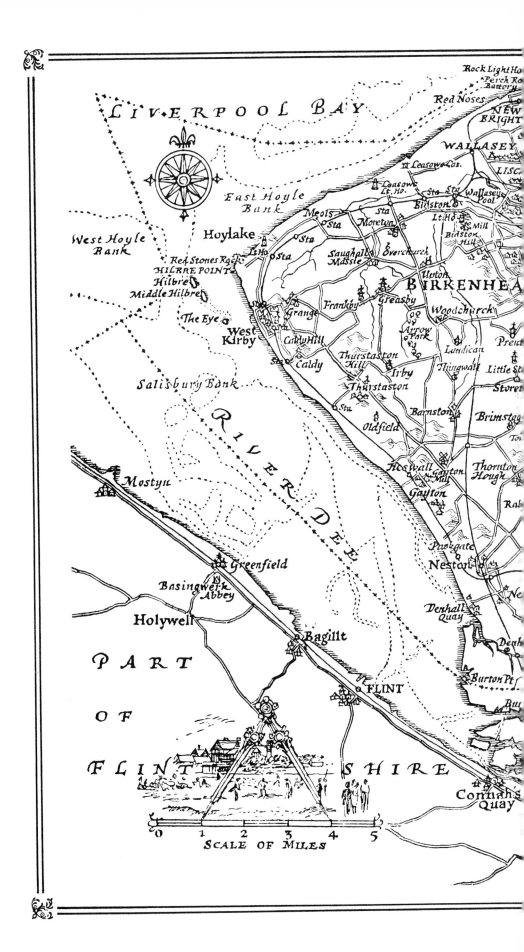

This map was originally drawn in the 1950s for the late Norman Ellison's book 'The Wirral Peninsula' and therefore does not include recent road improvements such as the M53 motorway

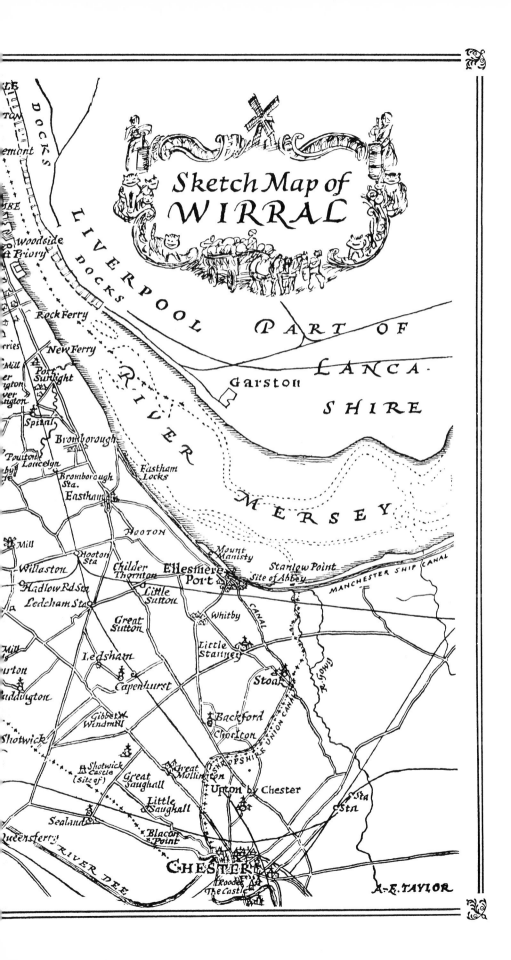

Sketch Map of
WIRRAL

A.E. TAYLOR

159

'God's croft,
twixt the Mersey and the Dee'